FREMDSPRACHENTEXTE · ENGLISCH

Tennessee Williams

A Streetcar Named Desire

von

sen

Philipp Reclam jun. Stuttgart

Diese Ausgabe darf nur in der Bundesrepublik Deutschland, in Österreich und in der Schweiz vertrieben werden.

Umschlagabbildung: Szenenfoto aus der Verfilmung des Dramas (1951) von Elia Kazan mit Vivien Leigh und Marlon Brando.

RECLAMS UNIVERSAL-BIBLIOTHEK Nr. 9240
Alle Rechte vorbehalten
Copyright für diese Ausgabe
© 1988 Philipp Reclam jun. GmbH & Co. KG, Stuttgart
Copyright für den Text
© 1947 by The University of the South
Renewed 1975 by The University of the South
Durchgesehene und bibliographisch ergänzte Ausgabe 2003
Gesamtherstellung: Reclam, Ditzingen. Printed in Germany 2012
RECLAM, UNIVERSAL-BIBLIOTHEK und RECLAMS
UNIVERSAL-BIBLIOTHEK sind eingetragene Marken
der Philipp Reclam jun. GmbH & Co. KG, Stuttgart
ISBN 978-3-15-009240-8

www.reclam.de

A Streetcar Named Desire

And so it was I entered the broken world
To trace the visionary company of love, its voice
An instant in the wind (I know not whither hurled)
But not for long to hold each desperate choice.

"The Broken Tower" by HART CRANE[1]

---

1 **streetcar:** Straßenbahn (1891 in New Orleans eingeführt, heute nur noch als Touristenattraktion auf der St. Charles Avenue betrieben).
Desire: 1. Stadtviertel von New Orleans; 2. Verlangen, Sehnsucht.
3 **to trace:** nachspüren.
visionary: visionär, eingebildet, unrealistisch.
4 **whither** (arch.): wohin.

The Characters

BLANCHE
STELLA
STANLEY
5 MITCH
EUNICE
STEVE
PABLO
A NEGRO WOMAN
10 A DOCTOR
A NURSE
A YOUNG COLLECTOR
A MEXICAN WOMAN
A TAMALE VENDOR

12 **collector:** Sammler, Einnehmer.
14 **tamale vendor:** Tamale-Verkäufer (*tamale:* mexikanisches Gericht, aus Hackfleisch, gestampftem Mais und Gewürzen zubereitet, in Mais-Hüllblätter eingewickelt und dann gedünstet).

Scene One

The exterior of a two-storey corner building on a street in
New Orleans which is named Elysian Fields² and runs
between the L&N tracks and the river. The section is poor
5 *but, unlike corresponding sections in other American*
cities, it has a raffish charm. The houses are mostly white
frame, weathered grey, with rickety outside stairs and gal-
leries and quaintly ornamented gables to the entrances of
both. It is first dark of an evening early in May. The sky
10 *that shows around the dim white building is a peculiarly*
tender blue, almost turquoise, which invests the scene with
a kind of lyricism and gracefully attenuates the atmo-
sphere of decay. You can almost feel the warm breath of
the brown river beyond the river warehouses with their

2 **two-storey:** zweigeschossig.
3 **Elysian Fields:** Elysische Gefilde; Straße in New Orleans (s. Stadtplan, S. 171).
4 **L & N tracks:** Schienen der »Louisville & Nashville«-Linie, die zwischen 1880 und 1890 nach New Orleans und Jacksonville (Fla.) ausge-
   baut wurde.
5 **section:** Stadtviertel.
6 **raffish:** verwegen, flott.
7 **frame:** hier: Haus mit Holzrahmen, Holzhaus.
   rickety: wackelig.
8 **quaintly** (adv.): altmodisch, seltsam.
   gable: Giebel.
11 **turquoise:** Türkis.
   to invest: ausstatten.
12 **to attenuate:** mildern, abschwächen.
14 **warehouse:** Lager, Speicher.

*faint redolences of bananas and coffee. A correspond-
ing air is evoked by the music of Negro entertainers at a
bar-room around the corner. In this part of New
Orleans you are practically always just around the*
5 *corner, or a few doors down the street, from a tinny
piano being played with the infatuated fluency of brown
fingers. This "Blue³ Piano" expresses the spirit of the
life which goes on here.*

Two women, one white and one coloured, are taking the
10 *air on the steps of the building. The white woman is
Eunice, who occupies the upstairs flat; the coloured
woman a neighbour, for New Orleans is a cosmopolitan
city where there is a relatively warm and easy intermingling of races in the old part of town.*
15 *Above the music of the "Blue Piano" the voices of people
on the street can be heard overlapping.*

NEGRO WOMAN *(to Eunice)* . . . she says St. Barnabas⁴
  would send out his dog to lick her and when he did
  she'd feel an icy cold wave all up an' down her. Well,
20 that night when —
A MAN *(to a Sailor)*. You keep right on going and you'll
  find it. You'll hear them tapping on the shutters.

---

1 **redolence:** Duft.
2 **to evoke:** hervorrufen.
5 **tinny:** blechern.
6 **infatuated:** vernarrt; hier: sich für den Nabel der Welt haltend.
7 **»Blue Piano«:** Blues-Klavier (New Orleans ist die Heimat des Jazz).
9f. **to take the air:** frische Luft schnappen.
13f. **intermingling:** Mischung.
16 **to overlap:** überlappen.
22 **to tap:** Step tanzen.
   shutter: Fensterladen.

SAILOR *(to Negro Woman and Eunice)*. Where's the Four
Deuces?

VENDOR. Red hot! Red hots!

NEGRO WOMAN. Don't waste your money in that clip joint!

5 SAILOR. I've got a date there.

VENDOR. Re-e-ed h-o-o-t!

NEGRO WOMAN. Don't let them sell you a Blue Moon
cocktail or you won't go out on your own feet!
(Two men come around the corner, Stanley Kowalski

10 *and Mitch. They are about twenty-eight or thirty years
old, roughly dressed in blue denim work clothes. Stanley carries his bowling jacket and a red-stained package
from a butcher's.)*

STANLEY *(to Mitch)*. Well, what did he say?

15 MITCH. He said he'd give us even money.

STANLEY. Naw! We gotta have odds!
(They stop at the foot of the steps.)

STANLEY *(bellowing)*. Hey, there! Stella, Baby!
(Stella comes out on the first-floor landing, a gentle

20 *young woman, about twenty-five, and of a background
obviously quite different from her husband's.)*

STELLA *(mildly)* Don't holler at me like that. Hi, Mitch.

---

1 f. **Four Deuces:** Wirtshausname, etwa: Zu den vier Zweien.
3 **red hot:** glühend heiß.
4 **clip joint:** Nepplokal.
5 **date:** Verabredung.
11 **denim:** Jeansstoff.
12 **bowling:** Kegeln (mit zehn Hölzern, auf gerader Bahn, mit schwerer, großer Kugel, die drei Grifflöcher aufweist).
15 **even money:** Wette, bei der die doppelte Einsatzsumme als Gewinn gezahlt wird.
16 **to have odds:** bessere Gewinnchancen haben (ungerades, also mindestens dreifaches Geld).
18 **to bellow:** brüllen.
22 **to holler** (infml.): schreien.

STANLEY. Catch!

STELLA. What?

STANLEY. Meat!

5   *(He heaves the package at her. She cries out in protest but manages to catch it: then she laughs breathlessly. Her husband and his companion have already started back around the corner.)*

STELLA *(calling after him)*. Stanley! Where are you going?

STANLEY. Bowling!

10   STELLA. Can I come watch?

STANLEY. Come on. *(He goes out.)*

STELLA. Be over soon. *(To the white woman.)* Hello, Eunice. How are you?

EUNICE. I'm all right. Tell Steve to get him a poor boy's

15   sandwich 'cause nothing's left here.

(They all laugh; the Coloured Woman does not stop. Stella goes out.)

COLOURED WOMAN. What was that package he th'ew at 'er? *(She rises from steps, laughing louder.)*

20   EUNICE. You hush, now!

NEGRO WOMAN. Catch *what!*

(She continues to laugh. Blanche comes around the corner, carrying a valise. She looks at a slip of paper, then at the building, then again at the slip and again

25   *at the building. Her expression is one of shocked disbelief. Her appearance is incongruous to this setting. She is daintily dressed in a white suit with a fluffy*

---

4 **to heave** (infml.): schmeißen.
20 **to hush** (auch: *to hush up* [infml.]): still sein.
23 **valise:** Reisetasche.
26 **incongruous:** wenig zusammenpassend.
27 **daintily** (adv.): elegant, geschmackvoll.
   suit: Kostüm.
   fluffy: flaumig.

bodice, necklace and earrings of pearl, white gloves and
hat, looking as if she were arriving at a summer tea or
cocktail party in the garden district. She is about five
years older than Stella. Her delicate beauty must avoid a
strong light. There is something about her uncertain
manner, as well as her white clothes, that suggests a
moth.)

EUNICE *(finally)*. What's the matter, honey? Are you
lost?

BLANCHE *(with faintly hysterical humour)*. They told me
to take a streetcar named Desire, and then transfer to
one called Cemeteries and ride six blocks and get off
at – Elysian Fields!

EUNICE. That's where you are now.

BLANCHE. At Elysian Fields?

EUNICE. This here is Elysian Fields.

BLANCHE. They mustn't have – understood – what
number I wanted . . .

EUNICE. What number you lookin' for?

(Blanche wearily refers to the slip of paper.)

BLANCHE. Six thirty-two.

EUNICE. You don't have to look no further.

BLANCHE *(uncomprehendingly)*. I'm looking for my sister, Stella DuBois. I mean – Mrs. Stanley Kowalski.

---

1 **bodice:** hier: Oberteil (des Kostüms).
3 **garden district:** schöne, vornehme Wohngegend in New Orleans, süd-
  westlich der Altstadt (Vieux Carré) aus dem 19. Jh. stammend.
7 **moth:** Motte.
8 **honey** (infml.): Schätzchen.
11 **to transfer:** umsteigen.
12 **Cemeteries:** Friedhöfe (Name einer Straßenbahnlinie in New Orleans; die Friedhöfe gehören zu den wichtigsten Sehenswürdigkeiten
   der Stadt).
23 **uncomprehendingly** (adv.): nicht verstehend, verständnislos.

EUNICE. That's the party. – You just did miss her, though.

BLANCHE. This – can this be – her home?

EUNICE. She's got the downstairs here and I got the up.

BLANCHE. Oh. She's – out?

5 EUNICE. You noticed that bowling alley around the corner?

BLANCHE. I'm – not sure I did.

EUNICE. Well, that's where she's at, watchin' her husband bowl.

10 *(There is a pause.)* You want to leave your suitcase here an' go find her?

BLANCHE. No.

NEGRO WOMAN. I'll go tell her you come.

BLANCHE. Thanks.

15 NEGRO WOMAN. You welcome. *(She goes out.)*

EUNICE. She wasn't expecting you?

BLANCHE. No. No, not tonight.

EUNICE. Well, why don't you just go in and make yourself at home till they get back.

20 BLANCHE. How could I – do that?

EUNICE. We own this place so I can let you in.

(She gets up and opens the downstairs door. A light goes on behind the blind, turning it light blue. Blanche slowly follows her into the downstairs flat. The sur-
25 *rounding areas dim out as the interior is lighted. Two rooms can be seen, not too clearly defined. The one first entered is primarily a kitchen but contains a folding bed to be used by Blanche. The room beyond this is a bed-room. Off this room is a narrow door to a bathroom.)*

---

5 **bowling alley:** hier: Gebäude mit Bowling-Bahnen.
23 **blind:** Jalousie.
25 **to dim out** (AE): verdunkeln, dunkel werden.

EUNICE *(defensively, noticing Blanche's look)*. It's sort of messed up right now but when it's clean it's real sweet.

BLANCHE. Is it?

EUNICE. Uh-huh, I think so. So you're Stella's sister?

5 BLANCHE. Yes. *(Wanting to get rid of her.)* Thanks for letting me in.

EUNICE. *Por nada*, as the Mexicans say, *por nada*! Stella spoke of you.

BLANCHE. Yes?

10 EUNICE. I think she said you taught school.

BLANCHE. Yes.

EUNICE. And you're from Mississippi, huh?

BLANCHE. Yes.

EUNICE. She showed me a picture of your home-place, the
15 plantation.

BLANCHE. Belle Reve?

EUNICE. A great big place with white columns.

BLANCHE. Yes . . .

EUNICE. A place like that must be awful hard to keep
20 up.

BLANCHE. If you will excuse me, I'm just about to drop.

EUNICE. Sure, honey. Why don't you set down?

BLANCHE. What I meant was I'd like to be left alone.

---

1 **sort of** (infml.): irgendwie.

2 **to mess up**: durcheinanderbringen.

7 **por nada** (Span.): für nichts und wieder nichts; hier: schon gut, macht nichts.

12 **Mississippi**: US-Bundesstaat, im Osten von Alabama, im Norden von Tennessee, im Westen von Arkansas und Louisiana und im Süden von Louisiana und dem Golf von Mexiko begrenzt.

14 **home-place**: Familiensitz.

16 **Belle Reve** (Fr.): richtig: *beau rêve*: schöner Traum; hier: Name einer Villa.

22 **to set**: *sit*.

EUNICE *(offended)*. Aw. I'll make myself scarce, in that
case.

BLANCHE. I didn't mean to be rude, but —

EUNICE. I'll drop by the bowling alley an' hustle her up.
5   *(She goes out of the door.)*
*(Blanche sits in a chair very stiffly with her shoulders
slightly hunched and her legs pressed close together and
her hands tightly clutching her purse as if she were quite
cold. After a while the blind look goes out of her eyes*
10   *and she begins to look slowly around. A cat screeches.
She catches her breath with a startled gesture. Suddenly
she notices something in a half opened closet. She
springs up and crosses to it, and removes a whisky bottle. She pours a half tumbler of whisky and tosses it*
15   *down. She carefully replaces the bottle and washes out
the tumbler at the sink. Then she resumes her seat in
front of the table.)*

BLANCHE *(faintly to herself)*. I've got to keep hold of
myself!
20   *(Stella comes quickly around the corner of the building
and runs to the door of the downstairs flat.)*

STELLA *(calling out joyfully)*. Blanche!

---

4 **to drop by:** vorbeischauen, kurz besuchen.
   to hustle s.o. up: jdn. drängen, zur Eile antreiben.
7 **hunched:** hochgezogen.
8 **to clutch:** festhalten, umklammern.
   purse: Handtasche (AE).
10 **to screech:** schreien.
11 **to catch one's breath:** den Atem (kurz) anhalten.
   gesture: Gebärde, Geste.
12 **closet:** Wandschrank.
14 **tumbler:** Wasserglas.
14f. **to toss down:** hinunterschütten.
18f. **to keep hold of o.s.:** etwa: sich nichts anmerken lassen, die Selbst-
   kontrolle behalten.

(For a moment they stare at each other. Then Blanche springs up and runs to her with a wild cry.)

BLANCHE. Stella, oh, Stella, Stella! Stella for Star!

(She begins to speak with feverish vivacity as if she feared for either of them to stop and think. They catch each other in a spasmodic embrace.) snob

BLANCHE. Now, then, let me look at you. But don't you look at me, Stella, no, no, no, not till later, not till I've bathed and rested! And turn that over-light off! Turn that off! I won't be looked at in this merciless glare! *(Stella laughs and complies.)* Come back here now! Oh, my baby! Stella! Stella for Star! *(She embraces her again.)* I thought you would never come back to this horrible place! What am I saying? I didn't mean to say that. I meant to be nice about it and say – Oh, what a convenient location and such – Ha-a-ha! Precious lamb! You haven't said a *word* to me.

STELLA. You haven't given me a chance to, honey! *(She laughs but her glance at Blanche is a little anxious.)*

BLANCHE. Well, now you talk. Open your pretty mouth and talk while I look around for some liquor! I know you must have some liquor on the place! Where could it be, I wonder? Oh, I spy, I spy!

---

1 **to stare at each other:** sich fest anschen, sich in die Augen sehen.
4 **vivacity:** Lebhaftigkeit.
5 **to catch:** hier: festhalten.
6 **spasmodic:** krampfartig.
9 **over-light:** (zu) grelles Licht.
10 **merciless:** gnadenlos, erbarmungslos.
  glare: grelles Licht.
11 **to comply:** sich fügen.
16 **location:** Lage.
21 **liquor:** Alkohol, Hochprozentiges, Schnaps.
23 **to spy:** sehen, erspähen.

(She rushes to the closet and removes the bottle; she is shaking all over and panting for breath as she tries to laugh. The bottle nearly slips from her grasp.)

STELLA *(noticing)*. Blanche, you sit down and let me pour
the drinks. I don't know what we've got to mix with.
Maybe a coke's in the icebox. Look'n see, honey,
while I'm —

BLANCHE. No coke, honey, not with my nerves tonight!
Where – where – where is —

STELLA. Stanley? Bowling! He loves it. They're having a –
found some soda! – tournament . . .

BLANCHE. Just water, baby, to chase it! Now don't get
worried, your sister hasn't turned into a drunkard,
she's just all shaken up and hot and tired and dirty!
You sit down, now, and explain this place to me! What
are you doing in a place like this?

STELLA. Now, Blanche —

BLANCHE. Oh, I'm not going to be hypocritical, I'm going
to be honestly critical about it! Never, never, never in
my worst dreams could I picture — Only Poe! Only
Mr. Edgar Allan Poe![5] – could do it justice! Out there I
suppose is the ghoul-haunted woodland of Weir! *(She
laughs.)*

---

2 **to pant for breath:** nach Luft schnappen.
6 **icebox:** Eisschrank.
11 **soda:** Mineralwasser.
   tournament: Turnier.
12 **to chase:** hier: nachspülen.
13 **drunkard:** Trinker(in), Trunkenbold.
14 **to be shaken up:** mitgenommen sein.
18 **hypocritical:** heuchlerisch.
21 **to do s.th. justice:** etwas würdigen.
22 **the ghoul-haunted woodland of Weir:** Refrain aus Edgar Allen Poes
   Gedicht *Ulalume* (1847) (*ghoul-haunted:* von Menschen mit schauri-
   gen Gelüsten heimgesucht; *Weir:* imaginäres Land in Poes Gedicht).

STELLA. No, honey, those are the L & N tracks.

BLANCHE. No, now seriously, putting joking aside. Why didn't you tell me, why didn't you write me, honey, why didn't you let me know?

5 STELLA *(carefully, pouring herself a drink)*. Tell you what, Blanche?

BLANCHE. Why, that you had to live in these conditions!

STELLA. Aren't you being a little intense about it? It's not that bad at all! New Orleans isn't like other

10 cities.

BLANCHE. This has got nothing to do with New Orleans. You might as well say – forgive me, blessed baby! *(She suddenly stops short.)* The subject is closed!

STELLA *(a little drily)*. Thanks.

15 *(During the pause, Blanche stares at her. She smiles at Blanche.)*

BLANCHE *(looking down at her glass, which shakes in her hand)*. You're all I've got in the world, and you're not glad to see me!

20 STELLA *(sincerely)*. Why, Blanche, you know that's not true.

BLANCHE. No? – I'd forgotten how quiet you were.

STELLA. You never did give me a chance to say much, Blanche. So I just got in the habit of being quiet

25 around you.

BLANCHE *(vaguely)*. A good habit to get into ... *(then abruptly.)* You haven't asked me how I happened to get away from the school before the spring term ended.

---

2 **to put aside:** beiseite lassen.

8 **to be intense about s.th.:** etwas zu ernst nehmen, etwas zu kritisch sehen.

26 **vaguely** (adv.): vage, unbestimmt.

STELLA. Well, I thought you'd volunteer that information – if you wanted to tell me.

BLANCHE. You thought I'd been fired?

STELLA. No, I – thought you might have – resigned. . . .

5 BLANCHE. I was so exhausted by all I'd been through my –
nerves broke. *(Nervously tamping cigarette.)* I was on
the verge of – lunacy, almost! So Mr. Graves – Mr.
Graves is the high school superintendent – he sug-
gested I take a leave of absence. I couldn't put all of
10 those details into the wire. . . . *(She drinks quickly.)*
Oh, this buzzes right through me and feels so *good*!

STELLA. Won't you have another?

BLANCHE. No, one's my limit.

STELLA. Sure?

15 BLANCHE. You haven't said a word about my appearance.

STELLA. You look just fine.

BLANCHE. God love you for a liar! Daylight never
exposed so total a ruin! But you – you've put on some
weight, yes, you're just as plump as a little partridge!
20 And it's so becoming to you!

---

1 **to volunteer:** freiwillig anbieten, freiwillig geben.
4 **to resign:** (Amt) niederlegen.
5 **to be through s.th.:** etwas mitgemacht haben.
6 **to tamp:** hier: fest ausdrücken.
7 **verge:** Rand.
   lunacy: Wahnsinn.
8 **high school superintendent:** Leiter einer High School (allgemeine
   Sekundarschule von Klasse 7 bis 12 für alle Schüler).
9 **leave of absence:** Beurlaubung.
11 **to buzz through one** (AE, slang): einem durchgehen.
18 **to expose:** entlarven, bloßstellen.
19 **plump:** mollig, gut genährt.
   partridge: Rebhuhn.
20 **to be becoming to s.o.:** jdm. gut stehen.

STELLA. Now, Blanche —

BLANCHE. Yes, it is, it is or I wouldn't say it! You just have
to watch around the hips a little. Stand up.

STELLA. Not now.

5 BLANCHE. You hear me? I said stand up! *(Stella complies
reluctantly.)* You messy child, you, you've spilt something on that pretty white lace collar! About your hair
– you ought to have it cut in a feather bob with your
dainty features. Stella, you have a maid, don't you?

10 STELLA. No. With only two rooms it's —

BLANCHE. What? *Two* rooms, did you say?

STELLA. This one and — *(She is embarrassed.)*

BLANCHE. The other one? *(She laughs sharply. There is an
embarrassed silence.)* How quiet you are, you're so

15 peaceful. Look how you sit there with your little hands
folded like a cherub in choir!

STELLA *(uncomfortably)*. I never had anything like your
energy, Blanche.

BLANCHE. Well, I never had your beautiful self-control. I

20 am going to take just one little tiny nip more, sort of to
put the stopper on, so to speak.   Then put the bottle
away so I won't be tempted *(She rises.)* I want you to
look at *my* figure! *(She turns around.)* You know I

---

6 **reluctantly** (adv.): widerwillig.
   messy: dreckig, schmutzig.
8 **feather bob:** luftiger Kurzhaarschnitt für Damen (ungleich lang
   geschnittene Haare, an den Enden leicht gelockt).
12 **embarrassed:** verlegen.
16 **cherub:** Cherub, Engelchen, Putte.
   choir: Chor.
17 **uncomfortably** (adv.): unbehaglich, mit Unbehagen.
20 **nip:** Schlückchen, Tröpfchen.
21 **to put the stopper on:** hier: (fig.) zum Abschluß; wörtl.: um den
   Stöpsel draufzusetzen.

haven't put on one ounce in ten years, Stella? I weigh
what I weighed the summer you left Belle Reve. The
summer Dad died and you left us . . .

STELLA *(a little wearily)*. It's just incredible, Blanche, how
5   well you're looking.

BLANCHE. You see I still have that awful vanity about my
looks even now that my looks are slipping! *(She laughs
nervously and glances at Stella for reassurance.)*

STELLA *(dutifully)*. They haven't slipped one particle.

10 BLANCHE. After all I've been through? You think I
believe that story? Blessed child! *(She touches her
forehead shakily.)* Stella, there's – only two rooms?

STELLA. And a bathroom.

BLANCHE. Oh, you do have a bathroom! First door to the
15 right at the top of the stairs? *(They both laugh uncomfortably.)* But, Stella, I don't see where you're going to
put me!

STELLA. We're going to put you in here.

BLANCHE. What kind of bed's this – one of those collaps-
20 ible things? *(She sits on it.)*

STELLA. Does it feel all right?

BLANCHE *(dubiously)*. Wonderful, honey. I don't like a
bed that gives much. But there's no door between the
two rooms, and Stanley – will it be decent?

25 STELLA. Stanley is Polish, you know.

---

1 **ounce:** Unze (28,35 g).
7 **to slip:** hier: nachlassen.
8 **reassurance:** Beruhigung.
9 **particle:** Fünkchen, bißchen.
19 f. **collapsible:** klappbar.
22 **dubiously** (adv.): zweifelnd.
23 **to give:** hier: nachgeben, weich sein (Matratze).
24 **decent:** anständig, schicklich.

snobish

BLANCHE. Oh, yes. They're something like Irish, aren't they?

STELLA. Well — rude

BLANCHE. Only not so – highbrow? *(They both laugh again in the same way.)* I brought some nice clothes to meet all your lovely friends in.

STELLA. I'm afraid you won't think they are lovely.

BLANCHE. What are they like?

STELLA. They're Stanley's friends.

BLANCHE. Polacks?

STELLA. They're a mixed lot, Blanche.

BLANCHE. Heterogeneous – types?

STELLA. Oh, yes. Yes, types is right!

BLANCHE. Well – anyhow – I brought nice clothes and I'll wear them. I guess you're hoping I'll say I'll put up at a hotel, but I'm not going to put up at a hotel. I want to be *near* you, got to be *with* somebody, I *can't* be *alone*! Because – as you must have noticed – I'm – *not* very *well*. . . . *(Her voice drops and her look is frightened.)*

STELLA. You seem a little bit nervous or overwrought or something.

BLANCHE. Will Stanley like me, or will I be just a visiting in-law, Stella? I couldn't stand that.

STELLA. You'll get along fine together, if you'll just try not to – well – compare him with men that we went out with at home.

---

4 **highbrow:** hochgestochen, intellektuell, anspruchsvoll.
10 **Polacks** (pej.): Polacken (Schimpfwort für Polen).
12 **heterogeneous:** heterogen, gemischt.
16 **to put up at a hotel:** in einem Hotel absteigen, wohnen.
20 **overwrought:** überreizt; auch: überfeinert.
23 **in-law:** hier: Schwägerin.
24 **to get along:** (mit jdm.) auskommen.

BLANCHE. Is he so – different? ~~apel / superman~~

STELLA. Yes. A different species.

BLANCHE. In what way; what's he like?

STELLA. Oh, you can't describe someone you're in love
with! Here's a picture of him! *(She hands a photograph
to Blanche.)*

BLANCHE. An officer?

STELLA. A Master Sergeant in the Engineers' Corps.
Those are decorations!

BLANCHE. He had those on when you met him?

STELLA. I assure you I wasn't just blinded by all the
brass.

BLANCHE. That's not what I —

STELLA. But of course there were things to adjust myself
to later on.

BLANCHE. Such as his civilian background! *(Stella laughs
uncertainly.)* How did he take it when you said I was
coming?

STELLA. Oh, Stanley doesn't know yet.

BLANCHE *(frightened)*. You – haven't told him?

STELLA. He's on the road a good deal.

BLANCHE. Oh. Travels?

STELLA. Yes.

BLANCHE. Good. I mean – isn't it?

---

2 **species:** Gattung.
8 **master sergeant:** Stabsfeldwebel (zweithöchster Unteroffiziersdienst-
grad).
 Engineers' Corps: Pioniertruppe.
9 **decoration:** Orden.
12 **brass:** 1. Messing (gemeint sind die Orden); 2. (slang) hohes Tier (bei
den Streitkräften).
14 **to adjust:** anpassen.
16 **civilian:** zivilistisch, Zivil-.

STELLA *(half to herself)*. I can hardly stand it when he is away for a night. . . .   ⟶ *opssessed*

BLANCHE. Why, Stella?

STELLA. When he's away for a week I nearly go wild!

5 BLANCHE. Gracious!

STELLA. And when he comes back I cry on his lap like a baby. . . . *(She smiles to herself.)*

BLANCHE. I guess that is what is meant by being in love. . . . *(Stella looks up with a radiant smile.)* Stella —

10 STELLA. What?

BLANCHE *(in an uneasy rush)*. I haven't asked you the things you probably thought I was going to ask. And so I'll expect you to be understanding about what *I* have to tell *you*.

15 STELLA. What, Blanche? *(Her face turns anxious.)*

BLANCHE. Well, Stella – you're going to reproach me, I know that you're bound to reproach me – but before you do – take into consideration – you left! I stayed and struggled! You came to New Orleans and looked

20 out for yourself! *I* stayed at *Belle Reve* and tried to hold it together! I'm not meaning this in any reproachful way, but *all* the burden descended on *my* shoulders.

STELLA. The best I could do was make my own living, Blanche.

25 *(Blanche begins to shake again with intensity.)*

BLANCHE. I know, I know. But you are the one that aban-

---

5 **Gracious!:** meine Güte!
9 **radiant:** strahlend.
11 **uneasy:** ängstlich; verlegen.
   rush: Drang, Anfall.
17 **to be bound to do s.th.:** etwas (zwangsläufig) tun müssen.
19f. **to look out for o.s.:** für sich selbst sorgen.
25 **intensity:** Heftigkeit.

doned Belle Reve, not I! I stayed and fought for it,
bled for it, almost died for it!

STELLA. Stop this hysterical outburst and tell me what's
happened? What do you mean fought and bled? What
kind of —

BLANCHE. I knew you would, Stella. I knew you would
take this attitude about it!

STELLA. About – what? – please!

BLANCHE *(slowly)*. The loss – the loss . . .

STELLA. Belle Reve? Lost, is it? No!

BLANCHE. Yes, Stella.
*(They stare at each other across the yellow-checked
linoleum of the table. Blanche slowly nods her head and
Stella looks slowly down at her hands folded on the
table. The music of the "blue piano" grows louder.
Blanche touches her handkerchief to her forehead.)*

STELLA. But how did it go? What happened?

BLANCHE *(springing up)*. You're a fine one to ask me how
it went!

STELLA. Blanche!

BLANCHE. You're a fine one to sit there *accusing me* of it!

STELLA. *Blanche!*

BLANCHE. I, I, *I* took the blows in my face and my body!
All of those deaths! The long parade to the graveyard!
Father, mother! Margaret, that dreadful way! So big
with it, it couldn't be put in a coffin! But had to be

---

3 **outburst:** Ausbruch.
12 **yellow-checked:** gelb kariert.
18 **You're a fine one** (iron.): Du bist mir die Richtige; ausgerechnet
du . . .
24 **graveyard:** Kirchhof, Friedhof.
25 **big:** hier vermutl.: hochschwanger.
26 **coffin:** Sarg.

burned like rubbish! You just came home in time for
the funerals, Stella. And funerals are pretty compared
to deaths. Funerals are quiet, but deaths – not always.
Sometimes their breathing is hoarse, and sometimes it
rattles, and sometimes they even cry out to you,
"Don't let me go!" Even the old, sometimes, say,
"Don't let me go." As if you were able to stop them!
But funerals are quiet, with pretty flowers. And, oh,
what gorgeous boxes they pack them away in! Unless
you were there at the bed when they cried out, "Hold
me!" you'd never suspect there was the struggle for
breath and bleeding. You didn't dream, but I saw!
Saw! Saw! And now you sit there telling me with your
eyes that I let the place go! How in hell do you think all
that sickness and dying was paid for? Death is expensive, Miss Stella! And old Cousin Jessie's right after
Margaret's, hers! Why, the Grim Reaper had put up
his tent on our doorstep! . . . Stella. Belle Reve was his
headquarters! Honey – that's how it slipped through
my fingers! Which of them left us a fortune? Which of
them left a cent of insurance even? Only poor Jessie –
one hundred to pay for her coffin. That was all, Stella!
And I with my pitiful salary at the school. Yes, accuse
me! Sit there and stare at me, thinking I let the place
go! *I* let the place go? Where were *you*. In bed with
your – Polack!   *obsessed about the
                    sexual relationship.*

1 **rubbish:** Abfall.
4 **hoarse:** heiser, rauh.
9 **gorgeous:** prächtig.
17 **the Grim Reaper:** der unerbittliche Schnitter (d. h. der Tod).
18 **doorstep:** Eingangsstufe.
19 **headquarters** (pl.): Hauptquartier.

STELLA *(springing)*. Blanche! You be still! That's enough!
   (She starts out.)

BLANCHE. Where are you going?

STELLA. I'm going into the bathroom to wash my face.

5 BLANCHE. Oh, Stella, Stella, you're crying!

STELLA. Does that surprise you?
   (Stella goes into the bathroom.)
   *(Outside is the sound of men's voices. Stanley, Steve
   and Mitch cross to the foot of the steps.)*

10 STEVE. And the old lady is on her way to Mass and she's
   late and there's a cop standin' in front of th' church an'
   she comes runnin' up an' says, "Officer – is Mass out
   yet?" He looks her over and says, "No, Lady, but y'r
   hat's on crooked!"⁶ *(They give a hoarse bellow of*
15 *laughter.)*

STEVE. Playing poker tomorrow night?

STANLEY. Yeah – at Mitch's.

MITCH. Not at my place. My mother's still sick. *(He starts
   off.)*

20 STANLEY *(calling after him)*. All right, we'll play at my
   place . . . but you bring the beer.

EUNICE *(hollering down from above)*. Break it up down
   there! I made the spaghetti dish and ate it myself.

STEVE *(going upstairs)*. I told you and phoned you we was
25 playing. *(To the men.)* Jax beer!

EUNICE. You never phoned me once.

---

11 **cop** (infml.): Schupo.
12 **Officer:** Herr Wachtmeister (Anrede).
13 **to look s.o. over:** jdn. von oben bis unten ansehen.
14 **crooked:** schief.
   bellow: Gebrüll.
25 **Jax beer:** amerikanische Biersorte.

STEVE. I told you at breakfast – and phoned you at lunch . . .

EUNICE. Well, never mind about that. You just get your-self home here once in a while.

5 STEVE. You want it in the papers? → *animalistic*

(More laughter and shouts of parting come from the men. Stanley throws the screen door of the kitchen open and comes in. He is of medium height, about five feet eight or nine, and strongly, compactly built. Animal joy
10 *in his being is implicit in all his movements and attitudes. Since earliest manhood the centre of his life has been pleasure with women, the giving and taking of it, not with weak indulgence, dependently, but with the power and pride of a* richly feathered male bird among
15 hens. *Branching out from this complete and satisfying centre are all the auxiliary channels of his life, such as his heartiness with men, his appreciation of rough humour, his love of good drink and food and games, his car, his radio, everything that is his, that bears his*
20 *emblem of the gaudy seed-bearer. He sizes women up at*

---

4 **once in a while:** ab und zu mal.
7 **screen door:** Fliegentür (Türrahmen mit Maschendrahtgeflecht).
8 **medium:** mittler(e, -er).
8 f. **five feet eight or nine:** etwa 1,73 m (1 foot = 0,3048 m; 1 inch = 2,54 cm).
9 **animal:** animalisch (hier nicht im negativen Sinn), kreatürlich.
10 **implicit:** enthalten.
13 **indulgence:** Nachgiebigkeit.
16 **auxiliary:** Hilfs-.
17 **heartiness:** Herzlichkeit.
   appreciation: Vorliebe.
20 **emblem:** Emblem, Sinnbild.
   gaudy: bunt, knallig, auffällig.
   seed-bearer: Samenträger.
   to size up: abschätzen.

*a glance, with sexual classifications, crude images flash-
ing into his mind and determining the way he smiles at
them.)*

BLANCHE *(drawing involuntarily back from his stare).*
5 You must be Stanley. I'm Blanche.

STANLEY. Stella's sister?

BLANCHE. Yes.

STANLEY. H'lo. Where's the little woman?

BLANCHE. In the bathroom.

10 STANLEY. Oh. Didn't know you were coming in town.

BLANCHE. I – uh —

STANLEY. Where you from, Blanche?

BLANCHE. Why, I – live in Laurel.

*(He has crossed to the closet and removed the whisky
15 bottle.)*

STANLEY. In Laurel, huh? Oh, yeah. Yeah, in Laurel,
that's right. Not in my territory. Liquor goes fast in hot
weather. *(He holds the bottle to the light to observe its
depletion.)* Have a shot?

20 BLANCHE. No, I – rarely touch it.

STANLEY. Some people rarely touch it, but it touches
them often.

BLANCHE *(faintly).* Ha-ha.

STANLEY. My clothes're stickin' to me. Do you mind if
25 I make myself comfortable? *(He starts to remove his
shirt.)*

---

1 **crude:** ordinär, grob.
4 **to draw back:** zurückweichen.
   involuntarily (adv.): unfreiwillig, unwillkürlich.
13 **Laurel:** Stadt im Staat Mississippi (220 km nordöstlich von New
   Orleans).
19 **depletion:** Entleerung.
   shot: Schuß (Whisky) (AE).

BLANCHE. Please, please do.

STANLEY. Be comfortable is my motto.

BLANCHE. It's mine, too. It's hard to stay looking fresh. I haven't washed or even powdered my face and – here you are!

STANLEY. You know you can catch cold sitting around in damp things, especially when you been exercising hard like bowling is. You're a teacher, aren't you?

BLANCHE. Yes.

STANLEY. What do you teach, Blanche?

BLANCHE. English.

STANLEY. I never was a very good English student. How long you here for, Blanche?

BLANCHE. I – don't know yet.

STANLEY. You going to shack up here?

BLANCHE. I thought I would if it's not inconvenient for you all.

STANLEY. Good.

BLANCHE. Travelling wears me out.

STANLEY. Well, take it easy.

(A cat screeches near the window. Blanche springs up.)

BLANCHE. What's that?

STANLEY. Cats. . . . Hey, Stella!

STELLA *(faintly, from the bathroom).* Yes, Stanley.

STANLEY. Haven't fallen in, have you? *(He grins at Blanche. She tries unsuccessfully to smile back. There is a silence.)* I'm afraid I'll strike you as being the un-refined type. Stella's spoke of you a good deal. You were married once, weren't you?

---

15 **to shack up** (infml.): zusammenziehen, zusammenwohnen.

16 **inconvenient:** ungelegen, unbequem.

27 f. **unrefined:** unkultiviert.

(The music of the polka rises up, faint in the distance.)
BLANCHE. Yes. When I was quite young.
STANLEY. What happened?
BLANCHE. The boy – the boy died. *(She sinks back down.)*
5   I'm afraid I'm – going to be sick!
(Her head falls on her arms.)

---

1 **polka:** Polka (urspr. lebhafter, böhmischer Tanz im ¾-Takt).

Scene Two

It is six o'clock the following evening. Blanche is bathing.
Stella is completing her toilette. Blanche's dress, a flower-
ed print, is laid out on Stella's bed.
Stanley enters the kitchen from outside, leaving the door
open on the perpetual "blue piano" around the corner.

STANLEY. What's all this monkey doings? → 'ord

STELLA. Oh, Stan! *(She jumps up and kisses him which he*
accepts with lordly composure.) I'm taking Blanche to
Galatoires' for supper and then to a show, because it's
your poker night.

STANLEY. How about my supper, huh? I'm not going to no
Galatoire's for supper!

STELLA. I put you a cold plate on ice. → expects to have food.

STANLEY. Well, isn't that just dandy!

STELLA. I'm going to try to keep Blanche out till the party
breaks up because I don't know how she would take it.

---

3 **toilette:** Toilette, (feine) Aufmachung, Kleidung.
4 **print:** hier: bedrucktes Kleid.
6 **perpetual:** fortwährend, ewig.
7 **What's all this monkey doings?** (pl.): Wozu die volle Montur? Wozu
   der ganze Stuß und Staat?
9 **composure:** Gelassenheit, Fassung.
10 **Galatoires':** vermutl. Name eines französischen Lokals in New
   Orleans.
14 **cold plate:** kalte Platte.
15 **dandy** (infml.): prima.

So we'll go to one of the little places in the Quarter afterwards and you'd better give me some money.

STANLEY. Where is she?

5 STELLA. She's soaking in a hot tub to quiet her nerves. She's terribly upset.

STANLEY. Over what?

STELLA. She's been through such an ordeal.

STANLEY. Yeah?

10 STELLA. Stan, we've – lost Belle Reve!

STANLEY. The place in the country?

STELLA. Yes.

STANLEY. How?

STELLA *(vaguely)*. Oh, it had to be – sacrificed or some-

15 thing. *(There is a pause while Stanley considers. Stella is changing into her dress.)* When she comes in be sure to say something nice about her appearance. And, oh! Don't mention the baby. I haven't said anything yet, I'm waiting until she gets in a quieter condition.

20 STANLEY *(ominously)*. So? ⟶ DOESn't Care

STELLA. And try to understand her and be nice to her, Stan.

BLANCHE *(singing in the bathroom)*.

"From the land of the sky blue water,

25   They brought a captive maid!"[7]

STELLA. She wasn't expecting to find us in such a small

1f. **Quarter:** französische Altstadt von New Orleans (Vieux Carré; s. Stadtplan, S. 171).

5 **to soak:** aufweichen.

tub: *bath tub:* Badewanne.

6 **upset:** aus der Fassung, nervös, mitgenommen.

8 **ordeal:** schwere Prüfung.

20 **ominously** (adv.): in unheilverkündendem Ton.

place. You see I'd tried to gloss things over a little in
my letters.

STANLEY. So?

STELLA. And admire her dress and tell her she's looking
5   wonderful. That's important with Blanche. Her little
weakness!

STANLEY. Yeah. I get the idea. Now let's skip back a little
to where you said the country place was disposed of.

STELLA. Oh! – yes . . .

10 STANLEY. How about that? Let's have a few more details
on that subject.

STELLA. It's best not to talk much about it until she's
calmed down. cora reference

STANLEY. So that's the deal, huh? Sister Blanche cannot
15 be annoyed with business details right now!

STELLA. You saw how she was last night.

STANLEY. Uh-hum, I saw how she was. Now let's have a
gander at the bill of sale.

STELLA. I haven't seen any.

20 STANLEY. She didn't show you no papers, no deed of sale
or nothing like that, huh?

STELLA. It seems like it wasn't sold.

STANLEY. Well, what in hell was it then, give away? To
charity?

25 STELLA. Shhh! She'll hear you.

---

1 **to gloss over:** beschönigen.
7 **to skip back:** (zu einem Thema) zurückspringen.
8 **to dispose of s.th.:** etwas verkaufen.
14 **that's the deal** (infml.): so steht der Handel, so steht es.
17 f. **to have a gander at s.th.** (infml.): mal etwas sehen lassen, mal lucki-lucki machen.
18 **bill of sale:** Verkaufsvertrag.
20 **deed of sale:** Übertragungsurkunde.

STANLEY. I don't care if she hears me. Let's see the papers!

STELLA. There weren't any papers, she didn't show any papers, I don't care about papers.

5 STANLEY. Have you ever heard of the Napoleonic code?

STELLA. No, Stanley, I haven't heard of the Napoleonic code and if I have, I don't see what it —

STANLEY. Let me enlighten you on a point or two, baby.

STELLA. Yes?

10 STANLEY. In the state of Louisiana we have the Napoleonic code according to which what belongs to the wife belongs to the husband and vice versa. For instance if I had a piece of property, or you had a piece of property —

15 STELLA. My head is swimming!

STANLEY. All right. I'll wait till she gets through soaking in a hot tub and then I'll inquire if *she* is acquainted with the Napoleonic code. It looks to me like you have been swindled, baby, and when you're swindled under

20 the Napoleonic code I'm swindled *too*. And I don't like to be *swindled*.

STELLA. There's plenty of time to ask her questions later but if you do now she'll go to pieces again. I don't understand what happened to Belle Reve but you

25 don't know how ridiculous you are being when you

---

5 **Napoleonic code:** Code Napoléon (französisches Zivilgesetzbuch).
8 **to enlighten:** aufklären, belehren.
10 **Louisiana:** südlicher Staat der USA am Mündungsdelta des Mississippi; größte Stadt von Louisiana ist New Orleans, die Hauptstadt ist Baton Rouge.
12 **vice versa:** und umgekehrt.
16 **to get through doing s.th.** (infml.): fertigwerden, etwas zu tun.
19 **to swindle:** beschwindeln, betrügen.
25 **ridiculous:** lächerlich.

family pride

suggest that my sister or I or anyone of our family
could have perpetrated a swindle on anyone else.

STANLEY. Then where's the money if the place was sold?

STELLA. Not sold – *lost, lost!*

(He stalks into bedroom, and she follows him.)
Stanley!
*(He pulls open the wardrobe trunk standing in middle
of room and jerks out an armful of dresses.)*

STANLEY. Open your eyes to this stuff! You think she got
them out of a teacher's pay?

fooled

STELLA. Hush!

seduced

STANLEY. Look at these feathers and furs that she come
here to preen herself in! What's this here? A solid-gold
dress, I believe! And this one! What is these here?
Fox-pieces! *(He blows on them.)* Genuine fox fur-
pieces, a half a mile long! Where are your fox-pieces,
Stella? Bushy snow-white ones, no less! Where are
your white fox-pieces?

STELLA. Those are inexpensive summer furs that Blanche
has had a long time.

STANLEY. I got an acquaintance who deals in this sort of
merchandise. I'll have him in here to appraise it. I'm
willing to bet you there's thousands of dollars invested
in this stuff here!

STELLA. Don't be such an idiot, Stanley!

powerful

2 **to perpetrate:** begehen.
5 **to stalk:** stolzieren; schleichen.
7 **wardrobe trunk:** Schrankkoffer.
8 **to jerk:** reißen.
13 **to preen o.s.:** sich putzen, sich brüsten.
   solid-gold: aus echtem Gold.
22 **merchandise:** Waren.
   to appraise: taxieren.

(He hurls the furs to the daybed. Then he jerks open a small drawer in the trunk and pulls up a fist-full of costume jewellery.)

STANLEY. And what have we here? The treasure chest of a
5   pirate!

STELLA. Oh, Stanley!

STANLEY. Pearls! Ropes of them! What is this sister of yours, a deep-sea diver who brings up sunken treasures? Or is she the champion safe-cracker of all time!
10 Bracelets of solid gold, too! Where are your pearls and gold bracelets? → lack of knowledge

STELLA. Shhh! Be still, Stanley!

STANLEY. And diamonds! A crown for an empress!

STELLA. A rhinestone tiara she wore to a costume ball.

15 STANLEY. What's rhinestone? Don't know

STELLA. Next door to glass.

STANLEY. Are you kidding? I have an acquaintance that works in a jewellery store. I'll have him in here to make an appraisal of this. Here's your plantation, or
20 what was left of it, here!

STELLA. You have no idea how stupid and horrid you're being! Now close that trunk before she comes out of the bathroom!

---

1 **daybed:** Ruhebett.
3 **costume jewellery:** Modeschmuck.
8 **deep-sea diver:** Tiefseetaucher.
9 **champion:** Meister-.
   safe-cracker: Safe-Knacker.
10 **bracelet:** Armband.
13 **empress:** Kaiserin.
14 **rhinestone tiara:** dreifache Krone aus unechten Edelsteinen.
17 **Are you kidding?** (slang): Machst du Witze?
19 **appraisal:** Abschätzung, Beurteilung.

(He kicks the trunk partly closed and sits on the kitchen table.)

STANLEY. The Kowalskis and the DuBois have different notions.

5 STELLA *(angrily)*. Indeed they have, thank heavens! – *I'm going outside. (She snatches up her white hat and gloves and crosses to the outside door.)* You come out with me while Blanche is getting dressed.

STANLEY. Since when do you give me orders?

10 STELLA. Are you going to stay here and insult her?

STANLEY. You're damn tootin' I'm going to stay here. *(Stella goes out on the porch. Blanche comes out of the bathroom in a red satin robe.)*

BLANCHE *(airily)*. Hello, Stanley! Here I am, all freshly
15 bathed and scented, and feeling like a brand new human being!

(He lights a cigarette.)

STANLEY. That's good.

BLANCHE *(drawing the curtains at the windows)*. Excuse
20 me while I slip on my pretty new dress!!

STANLEY. Go right ahead, Blanche.

(She closes the drapes between the rooms.)

BLANCHE. I understand there's to be a little card party to which we ladies are cordially *not* invited.

---

11 **You're damn tootin'** (AE, slang): Kannste aber laut sagen, kannste dich drauf verlassen.
12 **porch:** Veranda (AE).
13 **satin:** Satin, (Atlas-)Seide.
   robe: Morgenrock (AE).
14 **airily** (adv.): leichthin, blasiert.
15 **scented:** parfümiert.
22 **drapes:** Vorhänge, Gardinen.
24 **cordially** (adv.): herzlich.

STANLEY *(ominously)*. Yeah?
(Blanche throws off her robe and slips into a flowered print dress.)
BLANCHE. Where's Stella?
5 STANLEY. Out on the porch.
BLANCHE. I'm going to ask a favour of you in a moment.
STANLEY. What could that be, I wonder?   *gentle*
BLANCHE. Some buttons in back! You may enter!
10 *(He crosses through drapes with a smouldering look.)*
How do I look?
STANLEY. You look all right.
BLANCHE. Many thanks! Now the buttons!
STANLEY. I can't do nothing with them.
15 BLANCHE. You men with your big clumsy fingers. May I have a drag on your cig?
STANLEY. Have one for yourself.
BLANCHE. Why, thanks! . . . It looks like my trunk has exploded.
20 STANLEY. Me an' Stella were helping you unpack.
BLANCHE. Well, you certainly did a fast and thorough job of it!   *→ glossing over*
STANLEY. It looks like you raided some stylish shops in Paris.
25 BLANCHE. Ha-ha! Yes – clothes are my passion!
STANLEY. What does it cost for a string of fur-pieces like that?

---

10 **smouldering:** glühend, glimmend.
15 **clumsy:** unbeholfen.
16 **drag on your cig** (slang): Zug von deiner Kippe.
21 f. **to do a job of s.th.** (slang): etwas sauber hinkriegen.
23 **to raid:** überfallen, ausrauben.
   stylish: elegant, vornehm.

BLANCHE. Why, those were a tribute from an admirer of
  mine!

STANLEY. He must have had a lot of – admiration!

BLANCHE. Oh, in my youth I excited some admiration.
5 But look at me now! *(She smiles at him radiantly.)*
  Would you think it possible that I was once considered
  to be – attractive?

STANLEY. Your looks are okay.

BLANCHE. I was fishing for a compliment, Stanley.

10 STANLEY I don't go in for that stuff.

BLANCHE. What – stuff?

STANLEY. Compliments to women about their looks. I
  never met a woman that didn't know if she was good-
  looking or not without being told, and some of them
15 give themselves credit for more than they've got. I
  once went out with a doll who said to me, "I am the
  glamorous type, I am the glamorous type!" I said, "So
  what?"

BLANCHE. And what did she say then?

20 STANLEY. She didn't say nothing. That shut her up like a
  clam.

BLANCHE. Did it end the romance?

STANLEY. It ended the conversation – that was all. Some

---

1 **tribute:** Tribut, Zeichen der Anerkennung.
  admirer: Verehrer.
10 **to go in for s.th.:** für etwas zu haben sein.
15 **to give o.s. credit for s.th.:** sich für etwas (Gutes) halten, sich etwas
  zuschreiben.
17 **glamorous:** betörend.
17f. **so what?:** ja, und?
20f. **That shut her up like a clam:** Da hat sie kein Wort herausgebracht
  (*clam:* Muschel).
22 **romance:** Romanze, Liebesgeschichte.

men are took in by this Hollywood glamour stuff[8] and some men are not.

BLANCHE. I'm sure you belong in the second category.

STANLEY. That's right.

5 BLANCHE. I cannot imagine any witch of a woman casting a spell over you.

STANLEY. That's – right.

thick, stupid

BLANCHE. You're simple, straightforward and honest, a little bit on the primitive side I should think. To inter-

10 est you a woman would have to — (*She pauses with an indefinite gesture.*)

card references

STANLEY (*slowly*). Lay . . . her cards on the table.

BLANCHE (*smiling*). Yes – yes – cards on the table. . . . Well, life is too full of evasions and ambiguities, I

15 think. I like an artist who paints in strong, bold col-

simple ours, primary colours. I don't like pinks and creams and I never cared for wishy-washy people. That was why, when you walked in here last night, I said to myself –" My sister has married a man!" – Of course

20 that was all that I could tell about you.

STANLEY (*booming*). Now let's cut the re-bop[9]!

BLANCHE (*pressing hands to her ears*). Ouuuuu!

STELLA (*calling from the steps*). Stanley! You come out here and let Blanche finish dressing!

---

1 **to take s.o. in:** jdn. einnehmen, täuschen.
  glamour: Glanz.
5f. **to cast a spell over s.o.:** jdn. verzaubern, in seinen Bann ziehen.
14 **evasion:** Ausflucht.
  ambiguity: Mehrdeutigkeit.
16 **primary colours:** Grundfarben.
  cream: Cremefarbe, Pastellfarbe.
17 **wishy-washy:** wischi-waschi, saft- und kraftlos.
21 **to boom:** dröhnen.
  cut the re-bop: etwa: hör mit dem Mist auf, laß den Quatsch.

BLANCHE. I'm through dressing, honey.

STELLA. Well, you come out, then.

STANLEY. Your sister and I are having a little talk.

BLANCHE *(lightly)*. Honey, do me a favour. Run to the
5   drug-store and get me a lemon-coke with plenty of
chipped ice in it! – Will you do that for me, Sweetie?

STELLA *(uncertainly)*. Yes. *(She goes around the corner of
the building.)*

BLANCHE. The poor thing was out there listening to us,
10 and I have an idea she doesn't understand you as well
as I do. . . . All right; now, Mr. Kowalski, let us pro-
ceed without any more double-talk. I'm ready to answer all questions. I've nothing to hide. What is it?

STANLEY. There is such a thing in this State of Louisiana
15 as the Napoleonic code, according to which whatever
belongs to my wife is also mine – and vice versa.

BLANCHE. My, but you have an impressive judicial air!
*(She sprays herself with her atomizer; then playfully
sprays him with it. He seizes the atomizer and slams it
20 down on the dresser. She throws back her head and
laughs.)*

STANLEY. If I didn't know that you was my wife's sister I'd
get ideas about you!

5 **drug-store:** hier: Schnellimbiß.
6 **chipped:** klein gehackt.
   sweetie (infml.): *sweetheart:* Liebling.
12 **double-talk:** doppelzüngiges Gerede.
17 **My:** meine Güte!
   judicial: Richter-, richterlich.
   air: Miene, Aussehen.
18 **to spray:** besprühen.
   atomizer: Zerstäuber.
19f. **to slam s.th. down:** etwas hinknallen.
20 **dresser:** Frisierkommode (AE).

BLANCHE. Such as what?   → cards

STANLEY. Don't play so dumb. You know what! – Where's the papers?

BLANCHE. Papers?

5 STANLEY. Papers! That stuff people write on!

BLANCHE. Oh, papers, papers! Ha-ha! The first anniversary gift, all kinds of papers!

STANLEY. I'm talking of legal papers. Connected with the plantation.

10 BLANCHE. There *were* some papers.

STANLEY. You mean they're no longer existing?

BLANCHE. They probably are, somewhere.

STANLEY. But not in the trunk.

BLANCHE. Everything that I own is in that trunk.

15 STANLEY. Then why don't we have a look for them? *(He crosses to the trunk, shoves it roughly open and begins to open compartments.)*

BLANCHE. What in the name of heaven are you thinking of! What's in the back of that little boy's mind of 20 yours? That I am absconding with something, attempting some kind of treachery on my sister? – Let me do that! It will be faster and simpler. . . . *(She crosses to the trunk and takes out a box.)* I keep my papers mostly in this tin box. *(She opens it.)*

25 STANLEY. What's them underneath? *(He indicates another sheaf of paper.)*

---

2 **dumb** (AE, infml.): dumm, doof.

6 f. **anniversary:** Jahrestag; Hochzeitstag.

16 **to shove open:** aufstoßen.

17 **compartment:** Fach.

20 **to abscond:** sich aus dem Staub machen, durchbrennen.

25 **underneath:** unten, darunter.

26 **sheaf:** Bündel.

BLANCHE. These are love-letters, yellowing with antiquity, all from one boy. (*He snatches them up. She
speaks fiercely.*) Give those back to me!

STANLEY. I'll have a look at them first!

5 BLANCHE. The touch of your hands insults them!

STANLEY. Don't pull that stuff!

(*He rips off the ribbon and starts to examine them.
Blanche snatches them from him, and they cascade to
the floor.*)

10 BLANCHE. Now that you've touched them I'll burn them!

STANLEY (*staring, baffled*). What in hell are they?

BLANCHE (*on the floor gathering them up*). Poems a dead
boy wrote. I hurt him the way that you would like to
hurt me, but you can't! I'm not young and vulnerable

15 any more. But my young husband was and I – never
mind about that! Just give them back to me!

STANLEY. What do you mean by saying you'll have to burn
them?

BLANCHE. I'm sorry, I must have lost my head for a

20 moment. Everyone has something he won't let others
touch because of their – intimate nature. . . .

(*She now seems faint with exhaustion and she sits down
with the strong box and puts on a pair of glasses and
goes methodically through a large stack of papers.*)

1f. **antiquity:** Alter.
6 **Don't pull that stuff** (slang): Zieh nicht so 'ne Schau ab! Komm mir
nicht mit so'm Quatsch!
7 **to rip:** reißen.
8 **to cascade:** herabfallen, in allen Richtungen zu Boden fallen.
11 **baffled:** verblüfft, verwirrt.
14 **vulnerable:** verletzlich, verletzbar.
22 **exhaustion:** Erschöpfung.
23 **strong box:** Kassette.
24 **stack:** Stoß, Stapel.

Ambler & Ambler. Hmmmmm. ... Crabtree. ...
More Ambler & Ambler.

STANLEY. What is Ambler & Ambler?

BLANCHE. A firm that made loans on the place.

5 STANLEY. Then it *was* lost on a mortgage?

BLANCHE (*touching her forehead*). That must've been
what happened.

STANLEY. I don't want no ifs, ands or buts! What's all the
rest of them papers?

10 (*She hands him the entire box. He carries it to the table
and starts to examine the papers.*)

BLANCHE (*picking up a large envelope containing more
papers*). There are thousands of papers, stretching
back over hundreds of years, affecting Belle Reve as,

15 piece by piece, our improvident grandfathers and
father and uncles and brothers exchanged the land for
their epic fornications – to put it plainly! (*She removes
her glasses with an exhausted laugh.*) Till finally all that
was left – and Stella can verify that! – was the house

20 itself and about twenty acres of ground, including a
graveyard, to which now all but Stella and I have re-
treated. (*She pours the contents of the envelope on the
table.*) Here all of them are, all papers! I hereby endow
you with them! Take them, peruse them – commit

---

5 **mortgage:** Hypothek (Anleihe auf Haus- und Grundbesitz).
15 **improvident:** sorglos.
17 **fornication:** Unzucht, Hurerei.
19 **to verify:** bestätigen.
20 **acre:** Flächenmaß (0,4047 ha = 4047 m²).
23 **hereby:** hiermit.
  to endow: schenken.
24 **to peruse:** sorgfältig studieren.
24 f. **to commit s.th. to memory:** sich etwas einprägen.

them to memory, even! I think it's wonderfully fitting
that Belle Reve should finally be this bunch of old
papers in your big, capable hands! . . . I wonder if
Stella's come back with my lemon-coke. . . .

5 *(She leans back and closes her eyes.)*

STANLEY. I have a lawyer acquaintance who will study
these out.

BLANCHE. Present them to him with a box of aspirin tab-
lets.

10 STANLEY *(becoming somewhat sheepish).* You see, under
the Napoleonic code – a man has to take an interest in
his wife's affairs – especially now that she's going to
have a baby.

(Blanche opens her eyes. The "blue piano" sounds
15 *louder.)*

BLANCHE. Stella? Stella going to have a baby? *(Dreamily.)* I didn't know she was going to have a baby!

(She gets up and crosses to the outside door. Stella
appears around the corner with a carton from the drug-
20 *store.*

Stanley goes into the bedroom with the envelope and the
box. The inner rooms fade to darkness and the outside
wall of the house is visible.

Blanche meets Stella at the foot of the steps to the
25 *sidewalk.)*

BLANCHE. Stella, Stella for Star! How lovely to have a
baby! *(She embraces her sister. Stella returns the*
embrace with a convulsive sob. Blanche speaks softly.)

---

6 **lawyer:** Rechtsanwalt, Jurist.
10 **sheepish:** verlegen.
22 **to fade to darkness:** ausgeblendet werden.
25 **sidewalk:** Bürgersteig (AE).
28 **convulsive:** krampfartig.

Everything is all right; we thrashed it out. I feel a bit
shaky, but I think I handled it nicely. I laughed and
treated it all as a joke, called him a little boy and
laughed – and flirted! Yes – I was flirting with your
5 husband, Stella!

(Steve and Pablo appear carrying a case of beer.)
The guests are gathering for the poker party.
*(The two men pass between them, and with a short,
curious stare at Blanche, they enter the house.)*
10 STELLA. I'm sorry he did that to you.
BLANCHE. He's just not the sort that goes for jasmine
perfume! But maybe he's what we need to mix with
our blood now that we've lost Belle Reve and have to
go on without Belle Reve to protect us. . . . How pretty
15 the sky is! I ought to go there on a rocket that never
comes down.

(A Tamale Vendor calls out as he rounds the corner.)
VENDOR. Red hots! Red hots!
*(Blanche utters a sharp, frightened cry and shrinks
20 away; then she laughs breathlessly again.)*
BLANCHE. Which way do we – go now – Stella?
VENDOR. Re-e-d ho-o-ot!
BLANCHE. The blind are – leading the blind!
*(They disappear around the corner, Blanche's desper-
25 ate laughter ringing out once more.*
*Then there is a bellowing laugh from the interior of the
flat.*
*Then the "blue piano" and the hot[10] trumpet sound
louder.)*

---

1 **to thrash s.th. out:** etwas ausdiskutieren.
11 **to go for s.th.:** auf etwas aus sein, versessen sein.
19 f. **to shrink away:** zurückweichen.
28 **hot trumpet:** Trompete im Hot Jazz (s. Anm. 10).

Scene Three

formed in childhood ↗

The Poker Night.
There is a picture of Van Gogh's of a billiard-parlour at
night. The kitchen now suggests that sort of lurid noctur-
5 *nal brilliance, the raw colours of childhood's spectrum.*
Over the yellow linoleum of the kitchen table hangs an
electric bulb with a vivid green glass shade. The poker
players – Stanley, Steve, Mitch and Pablo – wear coloured
shirts, solid blues, a purple, a red-and-white check, a light
10 *green, and they are men at the peak of their physical man-*
hood, as coarse and direct and powerful as the primary
colours. There are vivid slices of watermelon on the table,
whisky bottles and glasses. The bedroom is relatively dim
with only the light that spills between the portières and
15 *through the wide window on the street.*
For a moment there is absorbed silence as a hand is dealt.

---

3 **billiard parlour:** Billardsaal.
4 **lurid:** gespenstisch, düster.
4f. **nocturnal:** nächtlich.
5 **brilliance:** Glanz, Pracht.
   raw: grell (AE).
   spectrum: (Farb-)Palette.
7 **bulb:** Glühbirne.
   vivid: leuchtend.
9 **solid:** hier: uni, einfarbig.
   blues (AE, sing.): hier: marineblau.
10 **peak:** Höhepunkt.
14 **to spill:** sich ergießen.
   portières: Vorhänge.
16 **to deal a hand:** ein Blatt (aus)geben (Karten).

jungle

STEVE. Anything wild this deal?

PABLO. One-eyed jacks are wild.[11]

STEVE. Give me two cards.

PABLO. You, Mitch?

5 MITCH. I'm out.

PABLO. One.

MITCH. Anyone want a shot?

STANLEY. Yeah. Me.

PABLO. Why don't somebody go to the Chinaman's and
10   bring back a load of chop suey?

STANLEY. Whem I'm losing you want to eat! Ante up!
    Openers? Openers! Get off the table, Mitch. Nothing
    belongs on a poker table but cards, chips and whisky.
    (He lurches up and tosses some watermelon rinds to the
15   *floor.)*

MITCH. Kind of on your high horse, ain't you?

STANLEY. How many?

STEVE. Give me three.

STANLEY. One.

20 MITCH. I'm out again. I oughta go home pretty soon.

STANLEY. Shut up.

---

1 **wild:** hier: beliebig verwendbar (wie ein Joker).
2 **one-eyed:** einäugig, nur im Profil zu sehen.
  jack: Bube.
9 **Chinaman:** hier: chinesisches Lokal.
10 **chop suey:** chinesisches Gericht (Eintopf aus Fleisch und Sojaboh-
  nensprossen; der Name ist aus dem Kantonesischen hergeleitet und
  bedeutet »Reste«).
11 **to ante up:** einsetzen, den Anfangseinsatz erhöhen.
13 **chips:** Spielmarken.
14 **to lurch up:** torkelnd aufstehen.
  rind: (Obst-)Schale, auch: (Käse-)Rinde.
16 **on one's high horse** (fig.): auf dem hohen Roß.
21 **to shut up** (infml.): die Klappe halten.

sensitive

MITCH. <u>I gotta sick mother.</u> She don't go to sleep until I
come in at night.

STANLEY. Then why don't you stay home with her?

MITCH. She says to go out, so I go, but I don't enjoy it. All
5   the while I keep wondering how she is.

STANLEY. Aw, for God's sake, go home, then!

PABLO. What've you got?

STEVE. Spade flush.

MITCH. You all are married. But I'll be alone when she
10   goes. – I'm going to the bathroom.

STANLEY. Hurry back and we'll fix you a sugar-tit.

MITCH. Aw, lay off. *(He crosses through the bedroom into
the bathroom.)*

STEVE *(dealing a hand).* Seven card stud.[12] *(Telling his
15   joke as he deals.)* This ole nigger is out in back of
his house sittin' down th'owing corn to the chickens
when all at once he hears a loud cackle and this young
hen comes lickety split around the side of the house
with the rooster right behind her and gaining on her
20   fast.

STANLEY *(impatient with the story).* Deal!

STEVE. But when the rooster catches sight of the nigger
th'owing the corn he puts on the brakes and lets the

4f. **all the while:** die ganze Zeit.
8 **spade flush:** Pik-Flush (fünf Pik-Karten).
11 **to fix** (infml.): hier: aufreißen, besorgen.
   sugar-tit (slang): Zucker-Titte, Mordsmieze.
12 **to lay off:** (mit etwas) aufhören, Schluß machen.
14 **seven card stud:** Sonderform des Pokers (s. Anm. 12).
17 **cackle:** Gegacker.
18 **lickety split** (AE, adv.): mit Volldampf.
19 **rooster:** Haushahn.
   to gain on s.o.: jdn. einholen.
23 **brake:** Bremse.

hen get away and starts pecking corn. And the old nigger says, "Lord God, I hopes I never gits *that* hongry!" ⟶ smutty joke

(Steve and Pablo laugh. The sisters appear around the corner of the building.)

STELLA. The game is still going on.

BLANCHE. How do I look?

STELLA. Lovely, Blanche.

BLANCHE. I feel so hot and frazzled. Wait till I powder before you open the door. Do I look done in?

STELLA. Why no. You are as fresh as a daisy.

BLANCHE. One that's been picked a few days.

(Stella opens the door and they enter.)

STELLA. Well, well, well. I see you boys are still at it!

STANLEY. Where you been?

STELLA. Blanche and I took in a show. Blanche, this is Mr. Gonzales and Mr. Hubbel.

BLANCHE. Please don't get up.   funny ⟵

STANLEY. Nobody's going to get up, so don't be worried.

STELLA. How much longer is this game going to continue?

STANLEY. Till we get ready to quit.

BLANCHE. Poker is so fascinating. Could I kibitz?

STANLEY. You could not. Why don't you women go up and sit with Eunice?

STELLA. Because it is nearly two-thirty. *(Blanche crosses*

---

1 **to peck:** picken.
9 **frazzled:** ausgefranst.
10 **done in:** fertig, geschafft.
11 **daisy:** Gänseblümchen.
14 **to be at s.th.:** bei etwas sein, mit etwas zugange sein.
16 **to take in:** noch mitnehmen.
21 **to quit:** (mit etwas) aufhören.
22 **to kibitz** (AE): kiebitzen (beim Kartenspiel zuschauen).

into the bedroom and partially closes the portières.)
Couldn't you call it quits after one more hand?
*(A chair scrapes. Stanley gives a loud whack of his hand
on her thigh.)* childish

5 STELLA *(sharply).* That's not fun, Stanley.
(The men laugh. Stella goes into the bedroom.)

STELLA. It makes me so mad when he does that in front of
people. Insulting / Reputation

BLANCHE. I think I will bathe.

10 STELLA. Again?

BLANCHE. My nerves are in knots. Is the bathroom oc-
cupied?

STELLA. I don't know.
(Blanche knocks. Mitch opens the door and comes out,
15 *still wiping his hands on a towel.)*

BLANCHE. Oh! – good evening.

MITCH. Hello. *(He stares at her.)*

STELLA. Blanche, this is Harold Mitchell. My sister,
Blanche DuBois.

20 MITCH *(with awkward courtesy).* How do you do, Miss
DuBois.

STELLA. How is your mother now, Mitch?

MITCH. About the same, thanks. She appreciated your
sending over that custard. – Excuse me, please.

---

1 **partially** (adv.); teilweise.
2 **to call it quits** (slang): etwas lassen, aufhören.
3 **to scrape:** rutschen, kratzen.
   whack: Klatsch, Schlag.
4 **thigh:** Oberschenkel.
11 **to be in knots:** sich verkrampfen.
20 **awkward:** linkisch.
   courtesy: Höflichkeit.
24 **custard:** Vanillesoße.

(He crosses slowly back into the kitchen, glancing back at Blanche and coughing a little shyly. He realizes he still has the towel in his hands and with an embarrassed laugh hands it to Stella. Blanche looks after him with a certain interest.)

BLANCHE. That one seems – superior to the others.

STELLA. Yes, he is.

BLANCHE. I thought he had a sort of sensitive look.

STELLA. His mother is sick.

BLANCHE. Is he married?

STELLA. No.

BLANCHE. Is he a wolf?

STELLA. Why, Blanche! *(Blanche laughs.)* I don't think he would be.

BLANCHE. What does – what does he do?

(She is unbuttoning her blouse.)

STELLA. He's on the precision bench in the spare parts department. At the plant Stanley travels for.

BLANCHE. Is that something much?

STELLA. No. Stanley's the only one of his crowd that's likely to get anywhere.

BLANCHE. What makes you think Stanley will?

STELLA. Look at him.

BLANCHE. I've looked at him.

STELLA. Then you should know.

BLANCHE. I'm sorry, but I haven't noticed the stamp of genius even on Stanley's forehead.

---

8 **sensitive:** feinfühlend, empfindsam, einfühlsam.
12 **wolf** (AE, slang): Schürzenjäger.
17 **precision bench:** Präzisionswerkbank.
   spare parts: Ersatzteile.
20 **crowd:** hier: Clique.
26 f. **stamp of genius:** Zeichen des Genies.

(She takes off the blouse and stands in her pink silk brassière and white skirt in the light through the portières. The game has continued in undertones.)

STELLA. It isn't on his forehead and it isn't genius.

BLANCHE. Oh. Well, what is it, and where? I would like to know.

STELLA. It's a drive that he has. You're standing in the light, Blanche! → Deliberetly?

BLANCHE. Oh, am I!

(She moves out of the yellow streak of light. Stella has removed her dress and put on a light blue satin kimono.)

STELLA *(with girlish laughter)*. You ought to see their wives.

BLANCHE *(laughingly)*. I can imagine. Big, beefy things, I suppose.

STELLA. You know that one upstairs? *(More laughter.)* One time *(laughing)* the plaster – *(laughing)* cracked —

STANLEY. You hens cut out that conversation in there!

STELLA. You can't hear us.

STANLEY. Well, you can hear me and I said to hush up!

STELLA. This is my house and I'll talk as much as I want to!

BLANCHE. Stella, don't start a row.

STELLA. He's half drunk! – I'll be out in a minute.

---

2 **brassière:** Büstenhalter.
3 **in undertones** (pl.): mit gedämpfter Stimme.
7 **drive:** Schwung.
10 **streak:** Streifen.
15 **beefy:** fleischig.
18 **plaster:** Putz (an Wänden und Decken).
20 **hen** (slang): ‚Huhn', Frau.
25 **row:** Krach, Streit.

*(She goes into the bathroom. Blanche rises and crosses
leisurely to a small white radio and turns it on.)*

STANLEY. Awright, Mitch, you in?

MITCH. What? Oh! – No, I'm out!

5 *(Blanche moves back into the streak of light. She raises
her arms and stretches, as she moves indolently back to
the chair.*

*Rhumba music comes over the radio. Mitch rises at the
table.)*

10 STANLEY. Who turned that on in there?

BLANCHE. I did. Do you mind?

STANLEY. Turn it off!

STEVE. Aw, let the girls have their music.

PABLO. Sure, that's good, leave it on!

15 STEVE. Sounds like Xavier Cugat![13]

*(Stanley jumps up and, crossing to the radio, turns it
off. He stops short at sight of Blanche in the chair. She
returns his look without flinching. Then he sits again at
the poker table.*

20 *Two of the men have started arguing hotly.)*

STEVE. I didn't hear you name it.

PABLO. Didn't I name it, Mitch?

MITCH. I wasn't listenin'.

PABLO. What were you doing, then?

25 STANLEY. He was looking through them drapes. *(He*

---

2 **leisurely** (adv.): gemächlich.
3 **in:** hier: drin (im Spiel).
6 **indolently** (adv.): träge, lässig.
8 **rhumba:** Tanz kubanischen Ursprungs im ¼-Takt mit stark ausge-
prägtem, synkopischen Rhythmus.
18 **to flinch:** (zurück)zucken.
21 **to name s.th.:** hier: (den Einsatz) bestimmen.

jumps up and jerks roughly at curtains to close them.)
Now deal the hand over again and let's play cards or
quit. Some people get ants when they win.
(Mitch rises as Stanley returns to his seat.)

5 STANLEY *(yelling)*. Sit down!

MITCH. I'm going to the "head". Deal me out.

PABLO. Sure he's got ants now. Seven five-dollar bills in
his pants pocket folded up tight as spitballs.

STEVE. Tomorrow you'll see him at the cashier's window
10 getting them changed into quarters.

STANLEY. And when he goes home he'll deposit them one
by one in a piggy bank his mother give him for Christmas *(Dealing.)* This game is Spit in the Ocean.[14]

(Mitch laughs uncomfortably and continues through
15 *the portières. He stops just inside.)*

BLANCHE *(softly)*. Hello! The Little Boys' Room is busy
right now.

MITCH. We've – been drinking beer.

BLANCHE. I hate beer.

20 MITCH. It's – a hot weather drink.

BLANCHE. Oh, I don't think so; it always makes me

---

3 **to get ants** (slang): unruhig werden, kein Sitzfleisch haben *(ant:*
Ameise).
5 **to yell:** schreien.
6 **head** (slang): Klo; eigtl.: Pütz (Toilette im Bug eines Schiffes).
to deal s.o. out: jdn. beim Kartengeben auslassen.
8 **pants** (pl.): Hose.
spitball: Papierkügelchen.
9 **cashier's window:** Kassenschalter.
10 **quarter:** Vierteldollar.
11 **to deposit:** einzahlen, hineinstecken.
12 **piggy bank:** Sparschwein.
16 **The Little Boys' Room:** Für kleine Jungs (Herrentoilette).
busy: besetzt.

warmer. Have you got any cigs? *(She has slipped on the dark red satin wrapper.)*

MITCH. Sure.

BLANCHE. What kind are they?

5 MITCH. Luckies.

BLANCHE. Oh, good. What a pretty case. Silver?

MITCH. Yes, Yes; read the inscription.

BLANCHE. Oh, is there an inscription? I can't make it out. *(He strikes a match and moves closer.)* Oh! *(Reading*
10 *with feigned difficulty.)*

> "And if God choose,
> I shall but love thee better – after – death!"[15]

Why, that's from my favourite sonnet[16] by Mrs. Browning!

15 MITCH. You know it?

BLANCHE. Certainly I do!

MITCH. There's a story connected with that inscription.

BLANCHE. It sounds like a romance.

MITCH. A pretty sad one.

20 BLANCHE. Oh?

MITCH. The girl's dead now.

BLANCHE *(in a tone of deep sympathy).* Oh!

MITCH. She knew she was dying when she give me this. A very strange girl, very sweet – very!

25 BLANCHE. She must have been fond of you. Sick people have such deep, sincere attachments.

shared history

---

2 **wrapper:** Morgenrock.
5 **Luckies** (pl.): Lucky Strike (amerikanische Zigarettenmarke).
7 **inscription:** Aufschrift.
10 **feigned:** vorgetäuscht.
12 **but** (adv.): bloß, (gerade) erst.
   thee (arch.): *you.*
13 **sonnet:** Sonett (s. Anm. 16).
26 **attachment:** Zuneigung.

MITCH. That's right, they certainly do.

BLANCHE. Sorrow makes for sincerity, I think.

MITCH. It sure brings it out in people.

BLANCHE. The little there is belongs to people who have
5 experienced some sorrow.

MITCH. I believe you are right about that.

BLANCHE. I'm positive that I am. Show me a person who
hasn't known any sorrow and I'll show you a shuperficial — Listen to me! My tongue is a little – thick! You
10 boys are responsible for it. The show let out at eleven
and we couldn't come home on account of the poker
game so we had to go somewhere and drink. I'm not
accustomed to having more than one drink. Two is the
limit – and *three*! *(She laughs.)* Tonight I had three.

15 STANLEY. Mitch!

MITCH. Deal me out. I'm talking to Miss —

BLANCHE. DuBois.

MITCH. Miss DuBois?

BLANCHE. It's a French name. It means woods and
20 Blanche means white, so the two together mean white
woods. Like an orchard in spring! You can remember
it by that.

MITCH. You're French?

BLANCHE. We are French by extraction. Our first Ameri-
25 can ancestors were French Huguenots. [17]

---

2 **to make for s.th.:** zu etwas beitragen.
  sincerity: Aufrichtigkeit.
7 **positive:** sicher.
8f. **shuperficial:** *superficial:* oberflächlich; die Schreibweise signalisiert
  die Aussprache »mit schwerer Zunge« (vgl. Z. 9).
10 **to let out** (AE): zu Ende sein.
11 **on account of:** wegen.
24 **extraction:** Abstammung.
25 **ancestor:** Vorfahre.

MITCH. You are Stella's sister, are you not?

BLANCHE. Yes, Stella is my precious little sister. I call her little in spite of the fact she's somewhat older than I. Just slightly. Less than a year. Will you do something for me?

MITCH. Sure. What?

BLANCHE. I bought this adorable little coloured paper lantern at a Chinese shop on Bourbon. Put it over the light bulb! Will you, please?

MITCH. Be glad to.

BLANCHE. I can't stand a naked light bulb, any more than I can a rude remark or a vulgar action.

MITCH (*adjusting the lantern*). I guess we strike you as being a pretty rough bunch.

BLANCHE. I'm very adaptable – to circumstances.

MITCH. Well, that's a good thing to be. You are visiting Stanley and Stella?

BLANCHE. Stella hasn't been so well lately, and I came down to help her for a while. She's very run down.

MITCH. You're not —?

BLANCHE. Married? No, no. I'm an old maid school-teacher!

MITCH. You may teach school but you're certainly not an old maid.

---

7 **adorable:** bezaubernd.
8 **Bourbon:** Kurzform von *Bourbon Street:* Straße in der Altstadt von New Orleans (s. Skizze).
12 **vulgar:** vulgär.
13 **to strike s.o. as . . .:** auf jdn. den Eindruck machen, als . . .
14 **bunch** (infml.): Haufen, Gruppe.
15 **adaptable:** anpassungsfähig.
18 **lately** (adv.): in jüngster Zeit.
19 **run down:** am Ende, heruntergekommen.

BLANCHE. Thank you, sir! I appreciate your gallantry!

MITCH. So you are in the teaching profession?

BLANCHE. Yes. Ah, yes . . .

MITCH. Grade school or high school or —

5 STANLEY *(bellowing)*. *Mitch!* Je lous?

MITCH. *Coming!*

BLANCHE. Gracious, what lung-power! . . . I teach high
school. In Laurel. game playing

MITCH. What do you teach? What subject?

10 BLANCHE. Guess! stereotypical

MITCH. I bet you teach art or music? *(Blanche laughs
delicately.)* Of course I could be wrong. You might
teach arithmetic.

BLANCHE. Never arithmetic, sir; never arithmetic! *(With a
15 laugh.)* I don't even know my multiplication tables!
No, I have the misfortune of being an English instructor. I attempt to instil a bunch of bobby-soxers and
drug-store Romeos with reverence for Hawthorne[18]
and Whitman[19] and Poe!

20 MITCH. I guess that some of them are more interested in
other things.

BLANCHE. How very right you are! Their literary heritage

---

1 **gallantry:** Galanterie.
4 **grade school:** Grundschule.
13 **arithmetic:** Rechnen.
15 **multiplication tables** (pl.): Einmaleins.
16f. **instructor:** Lehrer(in).
17 **to instil:** einflößen, beibringen.
   bobby-soxers (AE): Teenager, junge Mädchen (wegen der kurzen Söckchen, die sie tragen).
18 **Romeo:** Liebhaber (nach der männlichen Hauptfigur aus Shakespeares Liebestragödie *Romeo and Juliet*).
   reverence: Ehrfurcht.
22 **heritage:** Erbschaft, Erbe.

is not what most of them treasure above all else! But
they're sweet things! And in the spring, it's touching to
notice them making their first discovery of love! As if
nobody had ever known it before!

5 *(The bathroom door opens and Stella comes out.
Blanche continues talking to Mitch.)*
Oh! Have you finished? Wait – I'll turn on the radio.
*(She turns the knobs on the radio and it begins to play
"Wien, Wien, nur du allein." Blanche waltzes to the*

10 *music with romantic gestures. Mitch is delighted and
moves in awkward imitation like a dancing bear.
Stanley stalks fiercely through the portières into the bedroom. He crosses to the small white radio and snatches
it off the table. With a shouted oath, he tosses the instru-*

15 *ment out of the window.)*
STELLA. *Drunk – drunk – animal thing, you! (She rushes
through to the poker table.)* All of you – please go
home! If any of you have one spark of decency in
you—

20 BLANCHE *(wildly).* Stella, watch out, he's —
(Stanley charges after Stella.)
MEN *(feebly).* Take it easy, Stanley. Easy, fellow. – Let's
all —
STELLA. You lay your hands on me and I'll —

25 *(She backs out of sight. He advances and disappears.
There is the sound of a blow. Stella cries out. Blanche*

---

8 **knob:** Knopf.
9 **to waltz:** Walzer tanzen.
18 **decency:** Anstand.
20 **to watch out:** aufpassen.
21 **to charge after s.o.:** auf jdn. losgehen.
22 **take it easy:** immer mit der Ruhe.
25 **to back out of sight:** rückwärts außer Sicht gehen.

screams and runs into the kitchen. The men rush forward and there is grappling and cursing. Something is overturned with a crash.)

BLANCHE *(shrilly).* My sister is going to have a baby!

5 MITCH. This is terrible.

BLANCHE. Lunacy, absolute lunacy!

MITCH. Get him in here, men.

(Stanley is forced, pinioned by the two men, into the bedroom. He nearly throws them off. Then all at once

10 *he subsides and is limp in their grasp.*

They speak quietly and lovingly to him and he leans his face on one of their shoulders.) homo erotic

STELLA *(in a high, unnatural voice, out of sight).* I want to go away, I want to go away!

15 MITCH. Poker shouldn't be played in a house with women.

(Blanche rushes into the bedroom.)

BLANCHE. I want my sister's clothes! We'll go to that woman's upstairs!

MITCH. Where is the clothes?

20 BLANCHE *(opening the closet).* I've got them! *(She rushes through to Stella.)* Stella, Stella, precious! Dear, dear little sister, don't be afraid!

(With her arms around Stella, Blanche guides her to the outside doors and upstairs.)

25 STANLEY *(dully).* What's the matter; what's happened?

MITCH. You just blew your top, Stan.

PABLO. He's okay now.

---

2 **to grapple:** ringen.

3 **to overturn:** umstürzen, umfallen.

8 **to pinion:** fest (zwischen sich) halten, fest umklammern.

10 **to subside:** nachlassen, abklingen.

    limp: schlaff.

26 **to blow one's top:** in die Luft gehen, aus der Haut fahren.

STEVE. Sure, my boy's okay!

MITCH. Put him on the bed and get a wet towel.

PABLO. I think coffee would do him a world of good, now.

STANLEY *(thickly)*. I want water.

5 MITCH. Put him under the shower!

(The men talk quietly as they lead him to the bathroom.)

STANLEY. Let go of me, you sons of bitches!

(Sounds of blows are heard. The water goes on full tilt.)

10 STEVE. Let's get quick out of here!

(They rush to the poker table and sweep up their winnings on their way out.)

MITCH *(sadly but firmly)*. Poker should not be played in a house with women.

15 *(The door closes on them and the place is still. The Negro entertainers in the bar around the corner play "Paper Doll"[20] slow and blue. After a moment Stanley comes out of the bathroom dripping water and still in his clinging wet polka dot drawers.)*

20 STANLEY. Stella! *(There is a pause.)* My baby doll's left me!

(He breaks into sobs. Then he goes to the phone and dials, still shuddering with sobs.) feminine

Eunice? I want my baby! *(He waits a moment; then he*

---

3 **to do s.o. a world of good** (infml.): jdm. unheimlich gut tun.

8 **sons of bitches** (infml.): Hundesöhne.

9 **full tilt:** mit voller Wucht.

11 **to sweep up:** zusammenraffen.

17 **blue:** melancholisch.

18 **to drip:** (vor etwas) triefen.

19 **polka dot:** getupft.

   drawers (pl.): Unterhose.

23 **to dial:** (Telefonnummer) wählen.

   shuddering: sich schüttelnd.

hangs up and dials again.) Eunice! I'll keep on ringin'
until I talk with my baby!

*(An indistinguishable shrill voice is heard. He hurls
phone to floor. Dissonant brass and piano sounds as
the rooms dim out to darkness and the outer walls
appear in the night light. The "blue piano" plays for a
brief interval.*

*Finally, Stanley stumbles half-dressed out to the porch
and down the wooden steps to the pavement before the
building. There he throws back his head like a baying
hound and bellows his wife's name: "Stella! Stella,
sweetheart! Stella!")*

STANLEY. Stell-*lahhhhh*!

EUNICE *(calling down from the door of her upper apartment).* Quit that howling out there an' go back to
bed!   Sisterhood.

STANLEY. I want my baby down here. Stella, Stella!

EUNICE. She ain't comin' down so you quit! Or you'll git
th' law on you!

STANLEY. Stella!

EUNICE. You can't beat on a woman an' then call 'er back!
She won't come! And her goin' t' have a baby! . . . You
stinker! You whelp of a Polack, you! I hope they do

---

1 **to hang up:** (Hörer) auflegen.
3 **indistinguishable:** nicht unterscheidbar.
4 **dissonant:** dissonant, schrill klingend.
   brass: Blechbläser.
10 **to bay:** bellen, kläffen.
11 **hound:** Jagdhund.
14 f. **apartment:** Wohnung (AE).
18 f. **to git** (= *get*) **the law on o.s.:** (slang): die Polizei auf den Hals
   gehetzt kriegen.
23 **stinker** (infml.): ‚Ekel'.
   whelp (infml.): Hund.

haul you in and turn the fire hose on you, same as the
last time! happened before

STANLEY *(humbly)*. Eunice, I want my girl to come down
with me!

5   EUNICE. Hah! *(She slams her door.)*

STANLEY *(with heaven-splitting violence)*. STELL-
LAHHHHHH!
*(The low-tone clarinet moans. The door upstairs opens
again. Stella slips down the rickety stairs in her robe.*
10   *Her eyes are glistening with tears and her hair loose
about her throat and shoulders. They stare at each
other. Then they come together with low, animal
moans. He falls to his knees on the steps and presses his
face to her belly, curving a little with maternity. Her*
15   *eyes go blind with tenderness as she catches his head
and raises him level with her. He snatches the screen
door open and lifts her off her feet and bears her into the
dark flat.*
Blanche comes out on the upper landing in her robe and
20   *slips fearfully down the steps.)*

BLANCHE. Where is my little sister? Stella? Stella?
*(She stops before the dark entrance of her sister's flat.
Then catches her breath as if struck. She rushes down to
the walk before the house. She looks right and left as if*
25   *for sanctuary.*

---

1 **to haul in:** etwa: einlochen.
 fire hose: Feuerwehrschlauch.
8 **low-tone:** tief klingend.
 to moan: seufzen.
10 **to glisten:** glänzen.
14 **to curve:** sich wölben.
 maternity: Mutterschaft, Schwangerschaft.
16 **level with:** auf gleicher Höhe mit.
25 **sanctuary:** Zuflucht.

*The music fades away. Mitch appears from around the
corner.)*

MITCH. <u>Miss DuBois?</u> salvation

BLANCHE. Oh!

5 MITCH. All quiet on the Potomac now?

BLANCHE. She ran downstairs and went back in there with
him.

MITCH. Sure she did.

BLANCHE. I'm terrified!

10 MITCH. Ho-ho! There's nothing to be scared of. They're
crazy about each other.

BLANCHE. I'm not used to such —

MITCH. Naw, it's a shame this had to happen when you
just got here. But don't take it serious.

15 BLANCHE. Violence! Is so —

MITCH. Set down on the steps and have a cigarette with
me.

BLANCHE. I'm not properly dressed.

MITCH. That's don't make no difference in the Quarter.

20 BLANCHE. Such a pretty silver case.

MITCH. I showed you the inscription, didn't I?

BLANCHE. Yes. *(During the pause, she looks up at the
sky.)* There's so much – so much confusion in the
world. . . . *(He coughs diffidently.)* Thank you for

25 being so kind! I need kindness now.

---

5 **All quiet on the Potomac?:** etwa: Alles ruhig an der Front? (Zitat des
   Generals George McClellan [1826–85] aus dem amerikanischen Bür-
   gerkrieg; der Potomac fließt durch Washington [D.C.] und war einer
   der Hauptschauplätze dieses Kriegs).

24 **diffidently** (adv.): schüchtern, mißtrauisch.

Scene Four

It is early the following morning. There is a confusion of
street cries like a choral chant.
Stella is lying down in the bedroom. Her face is serene in
5 *the early morning sunlight. One hand rests on her belly,*
rounding slightly with new maternity. From the other
dangles a book of coloured comics. Her eyes and lips have
that almost narcotized tranquillity that is in the faces of
Eastern idols.
10 *The table is sloppy with remains of breakfast and the*
debris of the preceding night, and Stanley's gaudy
pyjamas lie across the threshold of the bathroom. The
outside door is slightly ajar on a sky of summer brilliance.
Blanche appears at this door. She has spent a sleepless
15 *night and her appearance entirely contrasts with Stella's.*
She presses her knuckles nervously to her lips as she looks
through the door, before entering.

---

3 **choral chant:** Choralgesang.
4 **serene:** heiter.
7 **to dangle:** baumeln.
8 **narcotized:** narkotisiert.
  tranquillity: Ruhe.
9 **Eastern idols:** orientalische Götzen, fernöstliche Götzen.
10 **sloppy:** schlampig, durcheinander.
   remains: Reste.
11 **debris:** Trümmer, Überbleibsel.
12 **threshold:** Schwelle.
13 **ajar:** einen Spalt offen.
16 **knuckle:** (Finger-)Knöchel.

BLANCHE. Stella?

STELLA *(stirring lazily)*. Hmmh?

*(Blanche utters a moaning cry and runs into the bed-
room, throwing herself down beside Stella in a rush of*
5   *hysterical tenderness.)*

BLANCHE. Baby, my baby sister!

STELLA *(drawing away from her)*. Blanche, what is the
matter with you?

(Blanche straightens up slowly and stands beside the
10   *bed looking down at her sister with knuckles pressed to*
her lips.)

BLANCHE. He's left?

STELLA. Stan? Yes.

BLANCHE. Will he be back?

15   STELLA. He's gone to get the car greased. Why?

BLANCHE. Why! I've been half crazy, Stella! When I
found out you'd been insane enough to come back in
here after what happened – I started to rush in after
you!

20   STELLA. I'm glad you didn't.

BLANCHE. What were you thinking of? *(Stella makes an
indefinite gesture.)* Answer me! What? What?

STELLA. Please, Blanche! Sit down and stop yelling.

BLANCHE. All right, Stella. I will repeat the question
25   quietly now. How could you come back in this place
last night? Why, you must have slept with him!

(Stella gets up in a calm and leisurely way.)

STELLA. Blanche, I'd forgotten how excitable you are.
You're making much too much fuss about this.

30   BLANCHE. Am I?

---

15 **to grease:** (Auto) abschmieren.

17 **insane:** wahnsinnig.

29 **fuss:** (fig.) Theater, Lärm.

STELLA. Yes, you are, Blanche. I know how it must have seemed to you and I'm awful sorry it had to happen, but it wasn't anything as serious as you seem to take it. In the first place, when men are drinking and playing
5   poker anything can happen. It's always a powder-keg. He didn't know what he was doing. . . . He was as good as a lamb when I came back and he's really very, very ashamed of himself.

BLANCHE. And that – that makes it all right?

10   STELLA. No, it isn't all right for anybody to make such a terrible row, but – people do sometimes.Stanley's always smashed things. Why, on our wedding night – soon as we came in here – he snatched off one of my slippers and rushed about the place smashing the light-
15   bulbs with it. violence

BLANCHE. He did – *what*?

STELLA. He smashed all the light-bulbs with the heel of my slipper! *(She laughs.)*

BLANCHE. And you – you *let* him? Didn't *run*, didn't
20   *scream*?

STELLA. I was – sort of – thrilled by it. *(She waits for a moment.)* Eunice and you had breakfast?

BLANCHE. Do you suppose I wanted any breakfast?

STELLA. There's some coffee left on the stove.

25   BLANCHE. You're so – matter of fact about it, Stella.

STELLA. What other can I be? He's taken the radio to get it fixed. It didn't land on the pavement so only one tube was smashed.

---

  5 **powder-keg:** Pulverfaß.
12 **to smash:** zerschlagen.
14 **slipper:** Hausschuh.
25 **matter of fact:** nüchtern, sachlich.
26f. **to get s.th. fixed:** etwas reparieren lassen.
28 **tube:** (Radio-)Röhre.

BLANCHE. And you are standing there smiling!

STELLA. What do you want me to do?

BLANCHE. Pull yourself together and face the facts.

STELLA. What are they, in your opinion?

5 BLANCHE. In my opinion? You're married to a madman!

STELLA. No!

BLANCHE. Yes, you are, your fix is worse than mine is!
   Only you're not being sensible about it. I'm going to
   do something. Get hold of myself and make myself a
10   new life!

STELLA. Yes?

BLANCHE. But you've given in. And that isn't right, you're
   not old! You can get out.

STELLA (*slowly and emphatically*). I'm not in anything I
15   want to get out of.

BLANCHE (*incredulously*). What – Stella?   proud of it

STELLA. I said I am not in anything that I have a desire to
   get out of. Look at the mess in this room! And those
   empty bottles! They went through two cases last night!

20 He promised this morning that he was going to quit
   having these poker parties, but you know how long
   such a promise is going to keep. Oh, well, it's his
   pleasure, like mine is movies and bridge. People have
   got to tolerate each other's habits, I guess.

25 BLANCHE. I don't understand you. (*Stella turns toward*

---

7 **fix** (infml.): Patsche, Klemme.
8 **sensible:** vernünftig.
14 **emphatically** (adv.): nachdrücklich.
16 **incredulously** (adv.): ungläubig.
18 **mess:** Durcheinander.
23 **movie** (AE): Film.
   bridge: Bridge (in England und Amerika weit verbreitetes Kartenspiel).

her.*) I don't understand your indifference. Is this a
Chinese philosophy you've – cultivated?

STELLA. Is what – what?

BLANCHE. This – shuffling about and mumbling – "One
tube smashed – beer-bottles – mess in the kitchen" – as
if nothing out of the ordinary has happened! *(Stella
laughs uncertainly and picking up the broom, twirls it in
her hands.)*

BLANCHE. Are you deliberately shaking that thing in my
face?

STELLA. No.

BLANCHE. Stop it. Let go of that broom. I won't have you
cleaning up for him!

STELLA. Then who's going to do it? Are you?

BLANCHE. I? I!

STELLA. No, I didn't think so.

BLANCHE. Oh, let me think, if only my mind would func-
tion! We've got to get hold of some money, that's the
way out!

STELLA. I guess that money is always nice to get hold of.

BLANCHE. Listen to me. I have an idea of some kind.
(Shakily she twists a cigarette into her holder.) Do you
remember Shep Huntleigh? *(Stella shakes her head.)*
Of course you remember Shep Huntleigh. I went out
with him at college and wore his pin for a while.
Well —

STELLA. Well?

---

4 **to shuffle about:** herumschlurfen.
   to mumble: murmeln.
6 **out of the ordinary:** außergewöhnlich.
7 **to twirl:** (hin- und her)drehen.
22 **holder:** *cigarette-holder:* Zigarettenspitze.
25 **to wear s.o.'s pin:** jds. Anstecknadel, Abzeichen tragen.

BLANCHE. I ran into him last winter. You know I went to
   Miami during the Christmas holidays?

STELLA. No.

BLANCHE. Well, I did. I took the trip as an investment,
5   thinking I'd meet someone with a million dollars.

STELLA. Did you?

BLANCHE. Yes. I ran into Shep Huntleigh – I ran into him
   on Biscayne Boulevard,[21] on Christmas Eve, about
   dusk . . . getting into his car – Cadillac convertible;
10   must have been a block long!

STELLA. I should think it would have been – inconvenient
   in traffic!

BLANCHE. You've heard of oil-wells?

STELLA. Yes – remotely.

15 BLANCHE. He has them, all over Texas. Texas is literally
   spouting gold in his pockets.

STELLA. My, my.

BLANCHE. Y'know how indifferent I am to money, I think
   of money in terms of what it does for you. But he could
20   do it, he could certainly do it!

STELLA. Do what, Blanche?

BLANCHE. Why – set us up in a – shop!

STELLA. What kind of a shop?

BLANCHE. Oh, a shop of some kind! He could do it with
25   half what his wife throws away at the races.

STELLA. He's married?

---

   9 **convertible:** Kabriolett.
 13 **oil-well:** Ölquelle.
 14 **remotely** (adv.): entfernt.
 16 **to spout:** spritzen, sprudeln.
 19 **in terms of . . .:** was . . . angeht.
 22 **to set up in a shop:** ein Geschäft einrichten.
 25 **race:** Pferderennen.

BLANCHE. Honey, would I be here if the man weren't married? *(Stella laughs a little. Blanche suddenly springs up and crosses to phone. She speaks shrilly.)* How do I get Western Union? – Operator! Western
5   Union!

STELLA. That's a dial phone, honey.

BLANCHE. I can't dial, I'm too —

STELLA. Just dial O.

BLANCHE. O?

10 STELLA. Yes, "O" for Operator! *(Blanche considers a moment; then she puts the phone down.)*

BLANCHE. Give me a pencil. Where is a slip of paper? I've got to write it down first – the message, I mean . . .
(She goes to the dressing-table, and grabs up a sheet of
15   *Kleenex and an eyebrow pencil for writing equipment.)*
Let me see now . . . *(She bites the pencil.)* "Darling Shep. Sister and I in desperate situation."

STELLA. I beg your pardon!

BLANCHE. "Sister and I in desperate situation. Will ex-
20   plain details later. Would you be interested in —?"
(She bites the pencil again.) "Would you be – interested – in . . ." *(She smashes the pencil on the table
and springs up.)* You never get anywhere with direct
appeals!

25 STELLA *(with a laugh)*. Don't be so ridiculous, darling!

BLANCHE. But I'll think of something, I've *got* to think of
– *some*thing! Don't, don't laugh at me, Stella! Please,
please don't – I – I want you to look at the contents of

---

4 **Western Union:** amerikanische Telegrammgesellschaft.
   operator: (Telefon-)Vermittlung.
14 **to grab up:** hastig aufnehmen.
14f. **sheet of Kleenex:** Papiertaschentuch (wie dt. »Tempo«).
15 **writing equipment:** Schreibmaterial.

my purse! Here's what's in it! *(She snatches her purse open.)* Sixty-five measly cents in coin of the realm!

STELLA *(crossing to bureau)*. Stanley doesn't give me a regular allowance, he likes to pay bills himself, but –
5 this morning he gave me ten dollars to smooth things over. You take five of it, Blanche, and I'll keep the rest.

BLANCHE. Oh, no. No, Stella.

STELLA *(insisting)*. I know how it helps your morale just
10 having a little pocket-money on you.

BLANCHE. No, thank you – I'll take to the streets!

STELLA. Talk sense! How did you happen to get so low on funds?

BLANCHE. Money just goes – it goes places. *(She rubs her
15 forehead.)* Sometime today I've got to get hold of a bromo!

STELLA. I'll fix you one now.

BLANCHE. Not yet – I've got to keep thinking!

STELLA. I wish you'd just let things go, at least for a –
20 while . . .

BLANCHE. Stella, I can't live with him! You can, he's your husband. But how could I stay here with him, after last night, with just those curtains between us?

STELLA. Blanche, you saw him at his worst last night.

---

2 **measly:** mager, mies.
  coin of the realm: Landeswährung.
3 **bureau:** Schreibtisch (AE).
4 **allowance:** hier: Haushaltsgeld.
5f. **to smooth things over:** die Sache wiedergutmachen, geradebiegen.
9 **morale:** Moral, innerer Halt.
11 **to take to the streets** (infml.): auf den Strich gehen.
12f. **low on funds** (pl.): knapp bei Kasse.
14 **to go places:** Ausflüge machen; hier: unter der Hand verschwinden.
16 **bromo** (infml.): Beruhigungstablette.

BLANCHE. On the contrary, I saw him at his best! What such a man has to offer is animal force and he gave a wonderful exhibition of that! But the only way to live with such a man is to – go to bed with him! And that's
5   your job – not mine!

STELLA. After you've rested a little, you'll see it's going to work out. You don't have to worry about anything while you're here. I mean – expenses . . .

BLANCHE. I have to plan for us both, to get us both – out!

10 STELLA. You take it for granted that I am in something that I want to get out of.

BLANCHE. I take it for granted that you still have sufficient memory of Belle Reve to find this place and these poker players impossible to live with.

15 STELLA. Well, you're taking entirely too much for granted.

BLANCHE. I can't believe you're in earnest.

STELLA. No?

BLANCHE. I understand how it happened – a little. You
20   saw him in uniform, an officer, not here but —

STELLA. I'm not sure it would have made any difference where I saw him.

BLANCHE. Now don't say it was one of those mysterious electric things between people! If you do I'll laugh in
25   your face.

STELLA. I am not going to say anything more at all about it!

BLANCHE. All right, then, don't!

STELLA. But there are things that happen between a man

---

3 **exhibition:** Vorführung.
7 **to work out:** funktionieren, klappen.
10 **to take s.th. for granted:** etwas für erwiesen halten.

and a woman in the dark – that sort of make everything
else seem – unimportant. *(Pause.)*

BLANCHE. What you are talking about is brutal desire –
just – Desire! – the name of that rattle-trap street-car

5 that bangs through the Quarter, up one old narrow
street and down another . . .

STELLA. Haven't you ever ridden on that street-car?

BLANCHE. It brought me here. – Where I'm not wanted
and where I'm ashamed to be . . .

10 STELLA. Then don't you think your superior attitude is a
bit out of place?

BLANCHE. I am not being or feeling at all superior, Stella.
Believe me I'm not! It's just this. This is how I look at
it. A man like that is someone to go out with – once –

15 twice – three times when the devil is in you. But live
with! Have a child by?

STELLA. I have told you I love him.

BLANCHE. Then I *tremble* for you! I just – *tremble* for
you. . . .

20 STELLA. I can't help your trembling if you insist on
trembling!

(There is a pause.)

BLANCHE. May I – speak – *plainly*?

STELLA. Yes, do. Go ahead. As plainly as you want to.

25 *(Outside, a train approaches. They are silent till the
noise subsides. They are both in the bedroom.
Under cover of the train's noise Stanley enters from
outside. He stands unseen by the women, holding some
packages in his arms, and overhears their following*

---

4 **rattle-trap** (infml.): Klapperkiste.
5 **to bang:** hier: scheppern.
11 **out of place:** fehl am Platz.
29 **to overhear:** mitanhören.

conversation. He wears an undershirt and grease-stained seersucker pants.)

BLANCHE. Well – if you'll forgive me – he's *common*!

STELLA. Why, yes, I suppose he is.

5 BLANCHE. Suppose! You can't have forgotten that much of our bringing up, Stella, that you just *suppose* that any part of a gentleman's in his nature! *Not one particle, no!* Oh, if he was just – *ordinary*! Just *plain* – but good and wholesome, but – *no*. There's something

10 downright – *bestial* – about him! You're hating me saying this, aren't you?

STELLA *(coldly)*. Go on and say it all, Blanche.

BLANCHE. He acts like an animal, has an animal's habits! Eats like one, moves like one, talks like one! There's

15 even something – sub-human – something not quite to the stage of humanity yet! Yes, something – ape-like about him, like one of those pictures I've seen in – anthropological studies! Thousands and thousands of years have passed him right by, and there he is – Stan-

20 ley Kowalski – survivor of the stone age! Bearing the raw meat home from the kill in the jungle! And you – *you* here – *waiting* for him! Maybe he'll strike you or

---

1 f. **grease-stained:** ölverschmiert, mit Ölflecken.

2 **seersucker:** Krepp(stoff) (leichtes Baumwollgewebe mit welliger Oberfläche).

9 **wholesome:** gesund.

10 **bestial:** bestialisch, tierisch.

15 **sub-human:** wie ein Untermensch.

16 **ape-like:** affenähnlich.

18 **anthropological:** anthropologisch (zur Lehre vom Menschen und seiner Entwicklung gehörig).

20 **survivor:** Überlebende(r).

21 **jungle:** Dschungel, Urwald.

maybe grunt and kiss you! That is, if kisses have been
discovered yet! Night falls and the other apes gather!
There in the front of the cave, all grunting like him,
and swilling and gnawing and hulking! His poker
night! – you call it – this party of apes! Somebody
growls – some creature snatches at something – the
fight is on! *God!* Maybe we are a long way from being
made in God's image, but Stella – my sister – there has
been *some* progress since then! Such things as art – as
poetry and music – such kinds of new light have come
into the world since then! In some kinds of people
some tenderer feelings have had some little beginning!
That we have got to make *grow!* And *cling* to, and hold
as our flag! In this dark march toward whatever it is
we're approaching ... *Don't – don't hang back with
the brutes!*

(*Another train passes outside. Stanley hesitates, licking
his lips. Then suddenly he turns stealthily about and
withdraws through front door. The women are still unaware of his presence. When the train has passed he
calls through the closed front door.*)

STANLEY. Hey! Hey, Stella!

STELLA (*who has listened gravely to Blanche*). Stanley!

BLANCHE. Stell, I

1 **to grunt:** grunzen.
2 **to fall:** hereinbrechen.
4 **to swill:** kippen, saufen.
 to gnaw: nagen.
 hulking: ungeschlacht.
6 **to growl:** brummen, knurren.
16 **brute:** brutaler Mensch.
18 **stealthily** (adv.): verstohlen.

(But Stella has gone to the front door. Stanley enters casually with his packages.)

STANLEY. Hiyuh, Stella, Blanche back?

STELLA. Yes, she's back.

5 STANLEY. Hiyuh, Blanche. *(He grins at her.)*

STELLA. You must've got under the car.

STANLEY. Them darn mechanics at Fritz's don't know their can from <u>third base</u>![22] CRUDE

(Stella has embraced him with both arms, fiercely, and
10 *full in the view of Blanche. He laughs and clasps her head to him. Over her head he grins through the curtains at Blanche.*

As the lights fade away, with a lingering brightness on their embrace, the music of the "blue piano" and trum-
15 *pet and drums is heard.)*

---

2 **casually** (adv.): 1. wie zufällig; 2. lässig.
7 **darn** (slang): *damned:* verdammt.
   mechanic: (Kfz-)Mechaniker.
7 f. **to know one's can from third base** (infml.): etwa: ein Klo vom dritten Mal unterscheiden (s. Anm. 22).

Scene Five

Blanche is seated in the bedroom fanning herself with a palm leaf as she reads over a just completed letter. Suddenly she bursts into a peal of laughter. Stella is dressing in the bedroom.

STELLA. What are you laughing at, honey?

BLANCHE. Myself, myself, for being such a liar! I'm writing a letter to Shep. *(She picks up the letter.)* "Darling Shep. I am spending the summer on the wing, making flying visits here and there. And who knows, perhaps I shall take a sudden notion to *swoop* down on *Dallas!* How would you feel about that? Ha-ha! *(She laughs nervously and brightly, touching her throat as if actually talking to Shep.)* Forewarned is forearmed, as they say!" – How does that sound?

STELLA. Uh-huh ...

BLANCHE *(going on nervously)*. "Most of my sister's friends go north in the summer but some have homes on the Gulf and there has been a continued round of entertainments, teas, cocktails, and luncheons —"

---

2 **to fan:** fächeln.
4 **peal of laughter:** schallendes Gelächter.
9 **on the wing:** im Flug.
11 **to take a notion:** Lust kriegen.
  to swoop down: einen Überraschungsangriff machen.
14 **Forewarned is forearmed** (prov.): etwa: Gefahr erkannt, Gefahr gebannt.
19 **the Gulf:** *Gulf of Mexico.*
20 **cocktail:** hier: Cocktail-Party.

*(A disturbance is heard upstairs at the Hubbels' apart-
ment.)*

STELLA *(crossing to the door).* Eunice seems to be having
some trouble with Steve.

5   *(Eunice's voice shouts in terrible wrath.)*

EUNICE. I heard about you and that blonde!

STEVE. That's a damn lie!

EUNICE. You ain't pulling the wool over my eyes! I
wouldn't mind if you'd stay down at the Four Deuces,
10   but you always going up.

STEVE. Who ever seen me up?

EUNICE. I seen you chasing her 'round the balcony – I'm
gonna call the vice squad!

STEVE. Don't you throw that at me!

15 EUNICE *(shrieking).* You hit me! I'm gonna call the
police!

*(A clatter of aluminium striking a wall is heard, fol-
lowed by a man's angry roar, shouts and overturned
furniture. There is a crash; then a relative hush.)*

20 BLANCHE *(brightly).* Did he *kill* her?

(Eunice appears on the steps in daemonic disorder.)

STELLA. No! She's coming downstairs.

EUNICE. Call the police, I'm going to call the police! *(She
rushes around the corner.)*

---

5 **wrath:** Zorn.
6 **blonde:** Blondine.
8 **to pull the wool over s.o.'s eyes** (infml.): jdm. Sand in die Augen
streuen.
13 **vice squad:** Sittenpolizei.
14 **to throw:** hier: (Karte) aufspielen, (mit einer Farbe, einem Blatt)
kommen.
17 **clatter:** Geschepper.
18 **roar:** Getöse, Lärm.
21 **daemonic:** dämonisch.

STELLA *(returning from the door).* Some of your sister's
friends have stayed in the city.
*(They laugh lightly. Stanley comes around the corner in
his green and scarlet silk bowling shirt. He trots up the
steps and bangs into the kitchen. Blanche registers his
entrance with nervous gestures.)*

STANLEY. What's a matter with Eun-uss?

STELLA. She and Steve had a row. Has she got the police?

STANLEY. Naw. She's gettin' a drink.

STELLA. That's much more practical! *Pragmatic*
*(Steve comes down nursing a bruise on his forehead
and looks in the door.)*

STEVE. *She here?*

STANLEY. Naw, naw. At the Four Deuces.

STEVE. That hunk! *(He looks around the corner a bit
timidly, then turns with affected boldness and runs after
her.)*

BLANCHE. I must jot that down in my notebook. Ha-ha!
I'm compiling a notebook of quaint little words and
phrases I've picked up here.

STANLEY. You won't pick up nothing here you ain't heard
before.

BLANCHE. Can I count on that?

STANLEY. You can count on it up to five hundred.

---

4 **scarlet:** scharlachrot.
  to trot: traben.
5 **to register:** registrieren, feststellen, bemerken.
11 **bruise:** Beule.
15 **hunk** (infml.): ‚Stück‘, Dreckstück.
16 **timidly** (adv.): schüchtern.
  affected: vorgetäuscht, gespielt.
18 **to jot down:** notieren.
19 **to compile:** zusammenstellen, zusammentragen.

BLANCHE. That's a mighty high number. *(He jerks open the bureau drawer, slams it shut and throws shoes in a corner. At each noise Blanche winces slightly. Finally she speaks.)* What sign were you born under?

5 STANLEY *(while he is dressing)*. Sign?

BLANCHE. Astrological sign. I bet you were born under Aries. Aries people are forceful and dynamic. They dote on noise! They love to bang things around! You must have had lots of banging around in the army, and

10 now that you're out, you make up for it by treating inanimate objects with such a fury!

(Stella has been going in and out of closet during this scene. Now she pops her head out of the closet.)

STELLA. Stanley was born just five minutes after Christ-

15 mas.

BLANCHE. Capricorn – the Goat![23]

STANLEY. What sign were *you* born under?

BLANCHE. Oh, my birthday's next month, the fifteenth of September; that's under Virgo.

20 STANLEY. What's Virgo?

BLANCHE. Virgo is the Virgin.

STANLEY *(contemptuously)*. *Hah!* *(He advances a little as he knots his tie.)* Say, do you happen to know somebody named Shaw?

---

3 **to wince:** zusammenzucken.
7 **Aries:** Widder (Sternbild, 22. März – 19. April).
8 **to dote:** abgöttisch lieben.
9 **to bang around** (infml.): sinnlos herumreisen, sinnlos herumrennen.
10 **to make up for s.th.:** etwas wiedergutmachen.
11 **inanimate:** unbelebt.
13 **to pop out:** schnell herausstrecken.
16 **Capricorn:** Steinbock (Sternbild, 22. Dezember – 19. Januar).
19 **Virgo:** Jungfrau (Sternbild, 23. August – 22. September).
22 **contemptuously** (adv.): verächtlich.

*(Her face expresses a faint shock. She reaches for the
cologne bottle and dampens her handkerchief as she
answers carefully.)*

BLANCHE. Why, everybody knows somebody named
Shaw! *got his facts together*

STANLEY. Well, this somebody named Shaw is under the
impression he met you in Laurel, but I figure he must
have got you mixed up with some other party because
this other party is someone he met at a hotel called the
Flamingo.

*(Blanche laughs breathlessly as she touches the co-
logne-dampened handkerchief to her temples.)*

BLANCHE. I'm afraid he does have me mixed up with this
"other party". The Hotel Flamingo is not the sort of
establishment I would dare to be seen in!

STANLEY. You know of it?

BLANCHE. Yes, I've seen it and smelled it.

STANLEY. You must've got pretty close if you could smell
it. *she knows*

BLANCHE. The odour of cheap perfume is penetrating.

STANLEY. That stuff you use is expensive?

BLANCHE. Twenty-five dollars an ounce! I'm nearly out.
That's just a hint if you want to remember my birthday! *(She speaks lightly but her voice has a note of
fear.)*

---

2 **cologne bottle:** Kölnisch-Wasser-Flasche.
7 **to figure** (AE, infml.): annehmen, glauben, schätzen.
8 **to mix up:** verwechseln.
   some other party (infml.): jd. anders.
12 **temple:** Schläfe.
20 **penetrating:** penetrant.
22 **to be out:** hier: nichts mehr haben.
24 **note:** Anflug, Unterton.

Threatening

STANLEY. Shaw must've got you mixed up. He goes in and
out of Laurel all the time, so he can check on it and
clear up any mistake. *Deadline*

(He turns away and crosses to the portières. Blanche
5   *closes her eyes as if faint. Her hand trembles as she lifts*
the handkerchief again to her forehead.
Steve and Eunice come around corner. Steve's arm is
around Eunice's shoulder and she is sobbing luxuri-
ously and he is cooing love-words. There is a murmur
10   *of thunder as they go slowly upstairs in a tight em-*
brace.)

STANLEY *(to Stella).* I'll wait for you at the Four Deuces!

STELLA. Hey! Don't I rate one kiss?

STANLEY. Not in front of your sister.

15   *(He goes out. Blanche rises from her chair. She seems*
faint; looks about her with an expression of almost
panic.)

BLANCHE. Stella! What have you heard about me?

STELLA. Huh?

20   BLANCHE. What have people been telling you about me?

STELLA. Telling?

BLANCHE. You haven't heard any – unkind – gossip about
me?

STELLA. Why, no, Blanche, of course not!

25   BLANCHE. Honey, there was – a good deal of talk in
Laurel.

STELLA. About *you*, Blanche?

---

2 **to check on s.th.:** etwas nachprüfen.
3 **to clear up:** klären, beseitigen.
8f. **luxuriously** (adv.): schwelgend.
9 **to coo:** gurren.
13 **to rate:** hier: verdienen.
22 **gossip:** Klatsch.

BLANCHE. I wasn't so good the last two years or so, after
Belle Reve had started to slip through my fingers.

STELLA. All of us do things we — *cuts her off*

BLANCHE. I never was hard or self-sufficient enough.
5 When people are soft – soft people have got to court
the favour of hard ones, Stella. Have got to be seductive – put on soft colours, the colours of butterfly
wings, and glow – make a little – temporary magic just
in order to pay for – one night's shelter! That's why
10 I've been – not so awf'ly good lately. I've run for protection, Stella, from under one leaky roof to another
leaky roof – because it was storm – all storm, and I was
– caught in the centre. . . . People don't see you – *men*
don't – don't even admit your existence unless they are
15 making love to you. And you've got to have your existence admitted by someone, if you're going to have
someone's protection. And so the soft people have got
to – shimmer and glow – put a – paper lantern over the
light. . . . But I'm scared now – awf'ly scared. I don't
20 know how much longer I can turn the trick. It isn't
enough to be soft. You've got to be soft *and attractive.*
And I – I'm fading now!
*(The afternoon has faded to dusk. Stella goes into the
bedroom and turns on the light under the paper lantern.
25 She holds a bottled soft drink in her hand.)*
Have you been listening to me?

---

4 **self-sufficient:** selbstgenügsam.
5 f. **to court the favour of s.o.:** um jds. Gunst buhlen.
6 f. **seductive:** verführerisch.
7 **butterfly:** Schmetterling.
11 **leaky:** leck, undicht.
18 **to shimmer:** schimmern, flimmern.
20 **to turn the trick:** etwas fertigbringen, etwas schaffen.
25 **bottled soft drink:** alkoholfreies Getränk in Flasche.

Blocks out what she doesn't want to hear

STELLA. I don't listen to you when you are being morbid!
  (She advances with the bottled coke.)

BLANCHE *(with abrupt change to gaiety)*. Is that coke for
  me?

5 STELLA. Not for anyone else!

BLANCHE. Why, you precious thing, you! Is it just coke?

STELLA *(turning)*. You mean you want a shot in it!

BLANCHE. Well, honey, a shot never does a coke any
  harm! Let me? You mustn't wait on me!

10 STELLA. I like to wait on you, Blanche. It makes it seem
  more like home. *(She goes into the kitchen, finds a
  glass and pours a shot of whisky into it.)*

BLANCHE. I have to admit I love to be waited on. . . .
  (She rushes into the bedroom. Stella goes to her with the
15 *glass. Blanche suddenly clutches Stella's free hand with
  a moaning sound and presses the hand to her lips. Stella
  is embarrassed by her show of emotion. Blanche speaks
  in a choked voice.)*

You're – you're – so *good* to me! And I —

20 STELLA. Blanche.

BLANCHE. I know, I won't! You hate me to talk senti-
  mental. But honey, *believe* I feel things more than I *tell*
  you! I *won't* stay long! I won't, I *promise* I —

STELLA. Blanche!

25 BLANCHE *(hysterically)*. I won't, I promise, *I'll* go! Go
  soon! I will *really*! I *won't* hang around until he –
  throws me out. . . .

STELLA. Now will you stop talking foolish?

---

1 **morbid:** morbide, krankhaft.
3 **gaiety:** Heiterkeit.
9 **to wait on s.o.:** jdn. bedienen.
18 **choked:** erstickt.

BLANCHE. Yes, honey. Watch how you pour – that fizzy
stuff foams over!
*(Blanche laughs shrilly and grabs the glass, but her
hand shakes so it almost slips from her grasp. Stella
pours the coke into the glass. It foams over and spills.
Blanche gives a piercing cry.)*
STELLA *(shocked by the cry)*. Heavens!
BLANCHE. Right on my pretty white skirt!
STELLA. Oh. . . . Use my hanky. Blot gently.
BLANCHE *(slowly recovering)*. I know – gently – gently . . .
STELLA. Did it stain?
BLANCHE. Not a bit. Ha-ha! Isn't that lucky? *(She sits
down shakily, taking a grateful drink. She holds the
glass in both hands and continues to laugh a little.)*
STELLA. Why did you scream like that?
BLANCHE. I don't know why I screamed! *(Continuing
nervously.)* Mitch – Mitch is coming at seven. I guess I
am just feeling nervous about our relations. *(She
begins to talk rapidly and breathlessly.)* He hasn't gotten a thing but a goodnight kiss, that's all I have given
him, Stella. I want his respect. And men don't want
anything they get too easy. But on the other hand men
lose interest quickly. Especially when the girl is over –
thirty. They think a girl over thirty ought to – the
vulgar term is – "put out." . . . And I – I'm not "putting
out." Of course he – he doesn't know – I mean I
haven't informed him – of my real age!
STELLA. Why are you sensitive about your age?

---

1 **fizzy:** sprudelnd.
2 **to foam over:** überschäumen.
9 **hanky:** Kurzform von *handkerchief:* Taschentuch.
   to blot: (ab)tupfen.
25 **to put out** (slang): es mit vielen treiben.

BLANCHE. Because of hard knocks my vanity's been given. What I mean is – he thinks I'm sort of – prim and proper, you know! *(She laughs out sharply.)* I want to *deceive* him enough to make him – want me. . . .

5 STELLA. Blanche, do you want *him*?

BLANCHE. I want to *rest*! I want to breathe quietly again! Yes – I *want* Mitch . . . *very badly*! Just think! If it happens! I can leave here and not be anyone's problem. . . .

10 *(Stanley comes around the corner with a drink under his belt.)*

STANLEY *(bawling)*. Hey, Steve! Hey, Eunice! Hey, Stella!

(There are joyous calls from above. Trumpet and
15 *drums are heard from around the corner.)*

STELLA *(kissing Blanche impulsively)*. It *will* happen!

BLANCHE *(doubtfully)*. It will?

STELLA. It will! *(She goes across into the kitchen, looking back at Blanche.)* It will, honey, *it will*. . . . But don't
20 take another drink! *(Her voice catches as she goes out of the door to meet her husband.)*

(Blanche sinks faintly back in her chair with her drink. Eunice shrieks with laughter and runs down the steps. Steve bounds after her with goat-like screeches and
25 *chases her around corner. Stanley and Stella twine arms as they follow, laughing.*
Dusk settles deeper. The music from the Four Deuces is slow and blue.)

2f. **prim and proper:** sittsam.
12 **to bawl:** brüllen.
20 **to catch:** hier: stocken.
24 **screech:** Kreischen.
25 **to twine arms:** Arme verschlingen.

BLANCHE. Ah, me, ah, me, ah, me . . .

(Her eyes fall shut and the palm leaf drops from her fingers. She slaps her hand on the chair arm a couple of times; then she raises herself wearily to her feet and picks up the hand mirror.)

(There is a little glimmer of lightning about the building.

The Negro Woman, cackling hysterically, swaying drunkenly, comes around the corner from the Four Deuces. At the same time, a Young Man enters from the opposite direction. The Negro Woman snaps her fingers before his belt.)

NEGRO WOMAN. Hey! Sugar!

(She says something indistinguishable. The Young Man shakes his head violently and edges hastily up the steps. He rings the bell. Blanche puts down the mirror. The Negro Woman has wandered down the street.)

BLANCHE. Come in.

(The Young Man appears through the portières. She regards him with interest.)

BLANCHE. Well, well! What can I do for *you*?

YOUNG MAN. I'm collecting for *The Evening Star*.

BLANCHE. I didn't know that stars took up collections.

YOUNG MAN. It's the paper.

BLANCHE. I know, I was joking – feebly! Will you – have a drink?

YOUNG MAN. No, ma'am. No, thank you. I can't drink on the job.

---

3 **to slap:** klapsen, leicht schlagen.

8 **to sway:** schwanken.

15 **to edge:** hier: sich (fort)stehlen.

23 **to take up:** hier: durchführen.

out of place

BLANCHE. Oh, well, now, let's see. ↖. No, I don't have a dime! I'm not the lady of the house. I'm her sister from Mississippi. I'm one of those poor relations you've heard about.

5 YOUNG MAN. That's all right. I'll drop by later. *(He starts to go out. She approaches a little.)*

BLANCHE. Hey! *(He turns back shyly. She puts a cigarette in a long holder.)* Could you give me a light? *(She crosses toward him. They meet at the door between the two rooms.)*

10

YOUNG MAN. Sure. *(He takes out a lighter.)* This doesn't always work.

BLANCHE. It's temperamental? *(It flares.)* Ah! Thank you.

15 YOUNG MAN. Thank *you!* *(He starts away again.)*

BLANCHE. Hey! *(He turns again, still more uncertainly. She goes close to him.)* What time is it?

YOUNG MAN. Fifteen of seven.

BLANCHE. So late? Don't you just love these long rainy

20   afternoons in New Orleans when an hour isn't just an hour – but a little bit of Eternity dropped in your hands – and who knows what to do with it?

YOUNG MAN. Yes, ma'am.

(In the ensuing pause, the "blue piano" is heard. It

25   *continues through the rest of this scene and the opening of the next. The Young Man clears his throat and looks glancingly at the door.)*

BLANCHE. You – uh – didn't get wet in the shower?

---

2 **dime** (AE, infml.): 10-Cent-Stück.
13 **to flare:** aufflackern.
18 **fifteen of seven** (AE): Viertel vor sieben.
24 **to ensue:** folgen.
26 **to clear one's throat:** sich räuspern.

YOUNG MAN. No, ma'am. I stepped inside.

BLANCHE. In a drug-store? And had a soda?

YOUNG MAN. Uhhuh.

BLANCHE. Chocolate?

5 YOUNG MAN. No, ma'am. Cherry.

BLANCHE. Mmmm!

YOUNG MAN. A cherry soda!

BLANCHE. You make my mouth water.   *reckless*

YOUNG MAN. Well, I'd better be —   *obsession with*

10 BLANCHE. Young man! Young, young, young, young – *age*
man! Has anyone ever told you that you look like a
young prince out of the Arabian Nights?

YOUNG MAN. No, ma'am.

(The Young Man laughs uncomfortably and stands like
15 *a bashful kid. Blanche speaks softly to him.)*

BLANCHE. Well, you do, honey lamb. Come here! Come
on over here like I told you! I want to kiss you – just
once – softly and sweetly on your mouth. *(Without
waiting for him to accept, she crosses quickly to him*
20 *and presses her lips to his.)* Run along now! It would be
nice to keep you, but I've got to be good and keep my
hands off children. Adios!

YOUNG MAN. Huh?

(He stares at her a moment. She opens the door for him
25 *and blows a kiss to him as he goes down the steps with a
dazed look. She stands there a little dreamily after he*

---

8 **to make s.o.'s mouth water:** jdm. den Mund wässerig machen.
12 **Arabian Nights:** Geschichten aus 1001 Nacht.
15 **bashful:** verschämt.
   kid (infml.): Kind.
22 **Adios** (Span.): Auf Wiedersehen.
25 **to blow s.o. a kiss:** jdm. eine Kußhand zuwerfen.
26 **dazed:** verwirrt.

has disappeared. Then Mitch appears around the corner with a bunch of roses.)

BLANCHE. Look who's coming! My Rosenkavalier![24] Bow to me first! Now present them.

(He does so. She curtsies low.)

Ahhh! Merciiii!

stereotypes

---

5 **to curtsy:** einen Knicks machen.
6 **merci** (Fr.): danke.

Scene Six

Williams

*It is about two a.m. the same night. The outer wall of the
building is visible. Blanche and Mitch come in. The utter
exhaustion which only a neurasthenic personality can*
5 *know is evident in Blanche's voice and manner. Mitch is
stolid but depressed. They have probably been out to the
amusement park on Lake Pontchartrain,[25] for Mitch is
bearing, upside down, a plaster statuette of Mae West,[26]
the sort of prize won at shooting-galleries and carnival*
10 *games of chance.*

BLANCHE *(stopping lifelessly at the steps)*. Well —
    (Mitch laughs uneasily)
    Well . . .
MITCH I guess it must be pretty late – and you're tired.
15 BLANCHE. Even the hot tamale man has deserted the
    street, and he hangs on till the end. *(Mitch laughs
    uneasily again.)* How will you get home?
MITCH. I'll walk over to Bourbon and catch an owl-
    car.

---

4 **neurasthenic:** nervenschwach.
6 **stolid:** phlegmatisch, stumpf.
  depressed: bedrückt.
8 **statuette:** kleine Statue.
9 **shooting-gallery:** Schießbude.
  carnival: hier: Kirmes.
10 **game of chance:** Glücksspiel.
18 f. **owl-car:** Straßenbahn für Nachtschwärmer.

BLANCHE *(laughing grimly)*. Is that street-car named Desire still grinding along the tracks at this hour?

MITCH *(heavily)*. I'm afraid you haven't gotten much fun out of this evening, Blanche.

5 BLANCHE. I spoiled it for *you*.

MITCH. No, you didn't, but I felt all the time that I wasn't giving you much – entertainment.

BLANCHE. I simply couldn't rise to the occasion. That was all. I don' think I've ever tried so hard to be gay and 10 made such a dismal mess of it. I get ten points for trying! – I *did* try.

MITCH. Why did you try if you didn't feel like it, Blanche?

BLANCHE. I was just obeying the law of nature.

MITCH. Which law is that?

15 BLANCHE. The one that says the lady must entertain the gentleman – or no dice! See if you can locate my door-key in this purse. When I'm so tired my fingers are all thumbs!

MITCH *(rooting in her purse)*. This it?

20 BLANCHE. No, honey, that's the key to my trunk which I must soon be packing.

MITCH. You mean you are leaving here soon?

BLANCHE. I've outstayed my welcome.

MITCH. This it?

25   *(The music fades away.)*

---

2 **to grind:** quietschend fahren.
8 **to rise to the occasion:** sich der Lage gewachsen zeigen.
10 **to make a mess of s.th.:** etwas verpatzen.
   dismal: trübe, schaurig.
16 **no dice** (infml.): nichts drin.
   to locate: lokalisieren, ausfindig machen.
19 **to root:** wühlen.
23 **to outstay one's welcome:** Gastfreundschaft überstrapazieren.

BLANCHE. Eureka![27] Honey, you open the door while I take a last look at the sky. *(She leans on the porch rail. He opens the door and stands awkwardly behind her.)* I'm looking for the Pleiades, the Seven Sisters, but these girls are not out tonight. Oh, yes they are, there they are! God bless them! All in a bunch going home from their little bridge party.... Y' get the door open? Good boy! I guess you – want to go now ... *(He shuffles and coughs a little.)*

MITCH. Can I – uh – kiss you – good night?

BLANCHE. Why do you always ask me if you may?

MITCH. I don't know whether you want me to or not.

BLANCHE. Why should you be so doubtful?

MITCH. That night when we parked by the lake and I kissed you, you —

BLANCHE. Honey, it wasn't the kiss I objected to. I liked the kiss very much. It was the other little – familiarity – that I – felt obliged to – discourage.... I didn't resent it! Not a bit in the world! In fact, I was somewhat flattered that you – desired me! But, honey, you know as well as I do that a single girl, a girl alone in the world, has got to keep a firm hold on her emotions or she'll be lost!

MITCH *(solemnly)*. Lost?

BLANCHE. I guess you are used to girls that like to be lost. The kind that get lost immediately, on the first date!

---

1 **Eureka** (Gr.): Ich hab's (s. Anm. 27).
4 **Pleiades:** Pleiaden (Sternbild aus sieben Sternen im Zeichen des Stiers).
17 **familiarity:** Vertraulichkeit.
18 **to resent:** übelnehmen.
22 **to keep a firm hold on s.th.:** etwas fest unter Kontrolle halten.
23 **lost:** hier: (moralisch) gefallen.

MITCH. I like you to be exactly the way that you are, because in all my – experience – I have never known anyone like you.

5 (*Blanche looks at him gravely; then she bursts into laughter and then claps a hand to her mouth.*)

MITCH. Are you laughing at me?

BLANCHE. No, honey. The lord and lady of the house have not yet returned, so come in. We'll have a night-cap. Let's leave the lights off. Shall we?

10 MITCH. You just – do what you want to.

(*Blanche precedes him into the kitchen. The outer wall of the building disappears and the interiors of the two rooms can be dimly seen.*)

BLANCHE (*remaining in the first room*). The other room's

15 more comfortable – go on in. This crashing around in the dark is my search for some liquor.

MITCH. You want a drink?

BLANCHE. I want *you* to have a drink! You have been so anxious and solemn all evening, and so have I; we have

20 both been anxious and solemn and now for these few last remaining moments of our lives together – I want to create – *joie de vivre*! I'm lighting a candle.

MITCH. That's good.

BLANCHE. We are going to be very Bohemian. We are

25 going to pretend that we are sitting in a little artists' cafe on the Left Bank in Paris! (*She lights a candle stub*

can't face reality

---

8 **night-cap:** Schlummertrunk.
15 **to crash around:** herumscheppern.
22 **joie de vivre** (Fr.): Lebensfreude.
24 **Bohemian:** wie Bohemiens, unkonventionell.
26 **Left Bank:** linkes Seine-Ufer.
   stub: Stummel.

and puts it in a bottle.) Je suis la Dame aux Camellias!
Vous êtes – Armand![28] Understand French?

MITCH *(heavily).* Naw. Naw, I —

BLANCHE. *Voulez-vous couchez avec moi ce soir? Vous ne*
comprenez pas? Ah, quel dommage! – I mean it's
a damned good thing. . . . I've found some liquor!
Just enough for two shots without any dividends,
honey . . .

MITCH *(heavily).* That's – good.

(She enters the bedroom with the drinks and the
candle.)

BLANCHE. Sit down! Why don't you take off your coat and
loosen your collar?

MITCH. I better leave it on.

BLANCHE. No. I want you to be comfortable.

MITCH. I am ashamed of the way I perspire. My shirt is
sticking to me.

BLANCHE. Perspiration is healthy. If people didn't perspire they would die in five minutes. *(She takes his coat*
from him.) This is a nice coat. What kind of material is
it?

MITCH. They call that stuff alpaca.

BLANCHE. Oh. Alpaca.

MITCH. It's very light weight alpaca.

1f. **Je suis la Dame aux Camellias** (richtig: *Camélias*) **. . . Armand!**
(Fr.): Ich bin die Kameliendame. Sie sind Armand!

4f. **Voulez-vous couchez** (richtig: *coucher*) **. . . quel dommage** (Fr.):
Wollen Sie heute abend mit mir schlafen? Verstehen Sie nicht? Oh,
wie schade!

7 **without any dividends** (pl.): ohne jeden Rest, ohne Nachschlag.

16 **to perspire:** schwitzen.

18 **perspiration:** Schweiß.

22 **alpaca:** Alpaka (dichtes Tuchgewebe aus Alpaka-Wolle, der Wolle
einer Lama-Art).

BLANCHE. Oh. Light weight alpaca.

MITCH. I don't like to wear a wash-coat even in summer
   because I sweat through it.

BLANCHE. Oh.

5 MITCH. And it don't look neat on me. A man with a heavy
   build has got to be careful of what he puts on him so he
   don't look too clumsy.

BLANCHE. You are not too heavy.

MITCH. You don't think I am?

10 BLANCHE. You are not the delicate type. You have a mas-
   sive bone-structure and a very imposing physique.

MITCH. Thank you. Last Christmas I was given a member-
   ship to the New Orleans Athletic Club.

BLANCHE. Oh, good.

15 MITCH. It was the finest present I ever was given. I work
   out there with the weights and I swim and I keep
   myself fit. When I started there, I was getting soft in
   the belly but now my belly is hard. It is so hard that
   now a man can punch me in the belly and it don't hurt
20 me. Punch me! Go on! See? *(She pokes lightly at him.)*

BLANCHE. Gracious. *(Her hand touches her chest.)*

MITCH. Guess how much I weigh, Blanche?

BLANCHE. Oh, I'd say in the vicinity of – one hundred and
   eighty?

25 MITCH. Guess again.

---

   2 **wash-coat** (AE): Flanellmantel.
   6 **build**: Körperbau, Figur.
  11 **imposing**: imposant.
      physique: Statur.
  13 **Athletic Club**: hier: Sportverein, Fitness-Verein.
  19 **to punch**: schlagen, boxen.
  20 **to poke**: stupsen.
  24 **in the vicinity of**: hier: so um (*vicinity*: Nähe, Nachbarschaft).

BLANCHE. Not that much?

MITCH. No. More.

BLANCHE. Well, you're a tall man and you can carry a good deal of weight without looking awkward.

5 MITCH. I weigh two hundred and seven pounds and I'm six feet one and one half inches tall in my bare feet – without shoes on. And that is what I weigh stripped.

BLANCHE. Oh, my goodness, me! It's awe-inspiring.

MITCH *(embarrassed)*. My weight is not a very interesting
10 subject to talk about. *(He hesitates for a moment.)* What's yours?

patronising

BLANCHE. My weight?

MITCH. Yes.

BLANCHE. Guess!

15 MITCH. Let me lift you.

BLANCHE. Samson! Go on, lift me. *(He comes behind her and puts his hand on her waist and raises her lightly off the ground.)* Well?

MITCH. You are light as a feather.

20 BLANCHE. Ha-ha! *(He lowers her but keeps his hands on her waist. Blanche speaks with an affectation of demureness.)* You may release me now.

MITCH. Huh?

BLANCHE *(gaily)*. I said unhand me, sir. *(He fumblingly*

southern belle.

---

5 **two hundred and seven pounds:** etwa 93 kg (1 pound = 453,59 g).

5 f. **six feet one and one half inches:** 1,84 m.

7 **stripped:** ausgezogen, nackt.

8 **awe-inspiring:** Ehrfurcht einflößend.

16 **Samson:** übermenschlich starker biblischer Held (Richter 14–16).

21 **affectation:** Verstellung, Heuchelei.

22 **demureness:** Sprödigkeit.

24 **to unhand** (hum.): freigeben, loslassen.

fumblingly (adv.): hier: ungeschickt.

embraces her. Her voice sounds gently reproving.)
Now, Mitch. Just because Stanley and Stella aren't at
home is no reason why you shouldn't behave like a
gentleman. *used to vilance*

5 MITCH. Just give me a slap whenever I step out of bounds.

BLANCHE. That won't be necessary. You're a natural
gentleman, one of the very few that are left in the
world. I don't want you to think that I am severe and
old maid school-teacherish or anything like that. It's

10 just – well —

MITCH. Huh?

BLANCHE. I guess it is just that I have – old-fashioned
bored ideals! *(She rolls her eyes, knowing he cannot see her
face. Mitch goes to the front door. There is a consider-*

15 *able silence between them. Blanche sighs and Mitch
coughs self-consciously.)*

MITCH *(finally)*. Where's Stanley and Stella tonight?

BLANCHE. They have gone out. With Mr. and Mrs. Hubbel upstairs.

20 MITCH. Where did they go?

BLANCHE. I think they were planning to go to a midnight
prevue at Loew's State.

MITCH. We should all go out together some night.

BLANCHE. No. That wouldn't be a good plan.

25 MITCH. Why not?

BLANCHE. You are an old friend of Stanley's?

---

1 **to reprove:** tadeln.
5 **slap:** Klaps, Schlag.
  to step out of bounds: Verbotenes tun.
22 **prevue:** nichtkommerzielle Vorab-Vorführung eines Films.
  Loew's State: Kino in der Canal Street, der Hauptstraße von New
Orleans.

MITCH. We was together in the Two-forty-first.

BLANCHE. I guess he talks to you frankly?

MITCH. Sure.

BLANCHE. Has he talked to you about me?

5 MITCH. Oh – not very much.

BLANCHE. The way you say that, I suspect that he has.

MITCH. No, he hasn't said much.

BLANCHE. But what he *has* said. What would you say his attitude toward me was?

10 MITCH. Why do you want to ask that?

BLANCHE. Well —

MITCH. Don't you get along with him?

BLANCHE. What do you think?

MITCH. I don't think he understands you.

15 BLANCHE. That is putting it mildly. If it weren't for Stella about to have a baby, I wouldn't be able to endure things here.

MITCH. He isn't – nice to you?

BLANCHE. He is insufferably rude. Goes out of his way to

20 offend me.

MITCH. In what way, Blanche?

BLANCHE. Why, in every conceivable way.

MITCH. I'm surprised to hear that.

BLANCHE. Are you?

25 MITCH. Well, I – don't see how anybody could be rude to you.

BLANCHE. It's really a pretty frightful situation. You see, there's no privacy here. There's just these portières

---

1 **Two-forty-first:** hier wohl: 241. Division.

19 **insufferably** (adv.): unerträglich.

  to go out of one's way: sich Mühe geben, Umstände machen.

22 **conceivable:** erdenklich.

28 **privacy:** Privatleben.

almost confesse [handwritten note]

between the two rooms at night. He stalks through the rooms in his underwear at night. And I have to ask him to close the bathroom door. That sort of commonness isn't necessary. You probably wonder why I don't
5 move out. Well, I'll tell you frankly. A teacher's salary is barely sufficient for her living-expenses. I didn't save a penny last year and so I had to come here for the summer. That's why I have to put up with my sister's husband. And he has to put up with me, apparently so
10 much against his wishes. . . . Surely he must have told you how much he hates me!

MITCH. I don't think he hates you.

hinting he likes her [handwritten note]

BLANCHE. He hates me. Or why would he insult me? Of course there is such a thing as the hostility of – perhaps
15 in some perverse kind of way he – No! To think of it makes me . . . *(She makes a gesture of revulsion. Then she finishes her drink. A pause follows.)*

MITCH. Blanche —

BLANCHE. Yes, honey?

20 MITCH. Can I ask you a question?

BLANCHE. Yes. What?

MITCH. How old are you?

(She makes a nervous gesture.)

BLANCHE. Why do you want to know?

25 MITCH. I talked to my mother about you and she said, "How old is Blanche?" And I wasn't able to tell her. *(There is another pause.)*

---

2 **underwear:** Unterwäsche.
6 **barely** (adv.): kaum.
   living-expenses (pl.): Lebensunterhalt.
8 **to put up with s.o.:** sich mit jdm. abfinden, jdn. ertragen.
14 **hostility:** Feindseligkeit.
16 **revulsion:** Widerwille, Ekel.

BLANCHE. You talked to your mother about me?

MITCH. Yes.

BLANCHE. Why?

MITCH. I told my mother how nice you were, and I liked
5   you.

BLANCHE. Were you sincere about that?

MITCH. You know I was.

BLANCHE. Why did your mother want to know my age?

MITCH. Mother is sick.

10   BLANCHE. I'm sorry to hear it. Badly?

MITCH. She won't live long. Maybe just a few months.

BLANCHE. Oh.

MITCH. She worries because I'm not settled.

BLANCHE. Oh.

15   MITCH. She wants me to be settled down before she —
     *(His voice is hoarse and he clears his throat twice,
     shuffling nervously around with his hands in and out of
     his pockets.)*

BLANCHE. You love her very much, don't you?

20   MITCH. Yes.

BLANCHE. I think you have a great capacity for devotion.
     You will be lonely when she passes on, won't you?
     (Mitch clears his throat and nods.) I understand what
     that is.

25   MITCH. To be lonley?

BLANCHE. I loved someone, too, and the person I loved I
     lost.

MITCH. Dead? *(She crosses to the window and sits on the
     sill, looking out. She pours herself another drink.)* A
30   man?

---

13 **to be settled:** hier: verheiratet sein.
22 **to pass on:** entschlafen, verscheiden.
29 **sill:** Fensterbrett.

BLANCHE. He was a boy, just a boy, when I was a very
young girl. When I was sixteen, I made the discovery –
love. All at once and much, much too completely. It
was like you suddenly turned a blinding light on something that had always been half in shadow, that's how it
struck the world for me. But I was unlucky. Deluded.
There was something different about the boy, a nerv-
ousness, a softness and tenderness which wasn't like
a man's, although he wasn't the least bit effeminate
looking – still – that thing was there. ... He came to
me for help. I didn't know that. I didn't find out anything till after our marriage when we'd run away and
come back and all I knew was I'd failed him in some
mysterious way and wasn't able to give the help he
needed but couldn't speak of! He was in the quick-
sands and clutching at me – but I wasn't holding him
out, I was slipping in with him! I didn't know that. I
didn't know anything except I loved him unendurably
but without being able to help him or help myself.
Then I found out. In the worst of all possible ways.
By coming suddenly into a room that I thought was
empty – which wasn't empty, but had two people in
it ... the boy I had married and an older man who
had been his friend for years ...

*(A locomotive is heard approaching outside. She claps
her hands to her ears and crouches over. The headlight
of the locomotive glares into the room as it thunders*

---

6 **to delude:** täuschen.
9 **effeminate:** verweichlicht.
13 **to fail s.o.:** jdn. enttäuschen, im Stich lassen.
15 f. **quicksand:** Treibsand.
26 **to crouch:** sich kauern.
    headlight: Scheinwerferlicht.
27 **to glare:** (grell) strahlen.

*past. As the noise recedes she straightens slowly and
continues speaking.)*

Afterwards we pretended that nothing had been
discovered. Yes, the three of us drove out to Moon
Lake Casino, very drunk and laughing all the way.

*(Polka music sounds, in a minor key faint with dis-
tance.)*

We danced the Varsouviana! Suddenly in the middle
of the dance the boy I had married broke away from
me and ran out of the casino. A few moments later – a
shot!

(The Polka stops abruptly.

*Blanche rises stiffly. Then the Polka resumes in a major
key.)*

I ran out – all did! – all ran and gathered about the
terrible thing at the edge of the lake! I couldn't get
near for the crowding. Then somebody caught my
arm. "Don't go any closer! Come back! You don't
want to see!" See? See what! Then I heard voices say –
Allan! Allan! The Grey boy! He'd stuck the revolver
into his mouth, and fired – so that the back of his head
had been – blown away! *sounds like gay*

(She sways and covers her face.)

It was because – on the dance-floor – unable to stop
myself – I'd suddenly said – "I know! I know! You

---

 1 **to recede:** zurückgehen.
 5 **Casino:** hier: Tanzlokal.
 6 **minor key:** Moll-Tonart.
 8 **Varsouviana:** ein der Mazurka ähnlicher Tanz im mäßig schnellen
    ¾-Takt.
13 f. **major key:** Dur-Tonart.
24 **dance-floor:** Tanzfläche.

moth – lost

disgust me . . ." And then the searchlight which had
been turned on the world was turned off again and
never for one moment since has there been any light
that's stronger than this – kitchen – candle. . . .

5   (*Mitch gets up awkwardly and moves towards her a
little. The Polka music increases. Mitch stands beside
her.*)

MITCH (*drawing her slowly into his arms*). You need
somebody. And I need somebody, too. Could it be –
10   you and me, Blanche? *clumsy proposal*
(*She stares at him vacantly for a moment. Then with a
soft cry huddles in his embrace. She makes a sobbing
effort to speak but the words won't come. He kisses her
forehead and her eyes and finally her lips. The Polka
15   tune fades out. Her breath is drawn and released in
long, grateful sobs.*)

BLANCHE. Sometimes – there's God – so quickly!

prayers answered

---

1 **to disgust:** anekeln.
   searchlight: Suchscheinwerfer.
11 **vacantly** (adv.): leer, ausdruckslos.
12 **to huddle:** sich kuscheln.

(degenerate - homosexual)

Scene Seven

It is late afternoon in mid-September.
The portières are open and a table is set for a birthday
supper, with cake and flowers.
5 *Stella is completing the decorations as Stanley comes in.*

STANLEY. What's all this stuff for?
STELLA. Honey, it's Blanche's birthday.
STANLEY. She here?
STELLA. In the bathroom.
10 STANLEY *(mimicking)*. "Washing out some things"?
STELLA. I reckon so.
STANLEY. How long she been in there?
STELLA. All afternoon.
STANLEY *(mimicking)*. "Soaking in a hot tub"?
15 STELLA. Yes.
STANLEY. Temperature 100 on the nose, and she soaks
    herself in a hot tub.
STELLA. She says it cools her off for the evening.
STANLEY. And you run out an' get her cokes, I suppose?
20   And serve 'em to Her Majesty in the tub? *(Stella*
    shrugs.) Set down here a minute.

---

10 **to mimic:** nachäffen, imitieren.
11 **to reckon:** schätzen, vermuten.
16 **100:** 100° Fahrenheit (= 38° Celsius; ungewöhnlich hohe Temperatur
    für New Orleans).
    on the nose (AE, infml.): spitz auf den Kopf.
21 **to shrug:** mit den Schultern zucken.

STELLA. Stanley, I've got things to do.

STANLEY. Set down! I've got th' dope on your big sister, Stella.

STELLA. Stanley, stop picking on Blanche.

5 STANLEY. That girl calls *me* common!

STELLA. Lately you been doing all you can think of to rub her the wrong way, Stanley, and Blanche is sensitive and you've got to realize that Blanche and I grew up under very different circumstances than you

10   did.

STANLEY. So I been told. And told and told and told! You know she's been feeding us a pack of lies here?

STELLA. No, I don't, and —

STANLEY. Well, she has, however. But now the cat's out

15   of the bag! I found out some things!

STELLA. What – things?

STANLEY. Things I already suspected. But now I got proof from the most reliable sources – which I have checked on!

20   *(Blanche is singing in the bathroom a saccharine popu-*
    lar ballad which is used contrapunctally with Stanley's
    speech.)

STELLA *(to Stanley).* Lower your voice!

STANLEY. Some canary-bird, huh!

25 STELLA. Now please tell me quietly what you think you've found out about my sister.

---

2 **I've got the dope on . . .** (slang): Ich weiß was über . . .
4 **to pick on s.o.:** auf jdm. herumhacken.
7 **to rub s.o. the wrong way** (infml.): (fig.) jdn. gegen das Fell streicheln, ärgern.
20 **saccharine:** zuckersüß, unecht und süßlich.
21 **contrapunctally** (adv.): kontrapunktisch.
24 **canary-bird:** Kanarienvogel; Sängerin.

[handwritten annotation: setting oot his case]

STANLEY. Lie Number One: All this squeamishness she puts on! You should just know the line she's been feeding to Mitch. He thought she had never been more than kissed by a fellow! But Sister Blanche is no lily!

5 Ha-ha! Some lily she is! *[handwritten: white]*

STELLA. What have you heard and who from?

STANLEY. Our supply-man down at the plant has been going through Laurel for years and he knows all about her and everybody else in the town of Laurel knows all

10 about her. She is as famous in Laurel as if she was the President of the United States, only she is not respected by any party! This supply-man stops at a hotel called the Flamingo.

BLANCHE *(singing blithely)*.

15   "Say, it's only a paper moon,
      Sailing over a cardboard sea
      – But it wouldn't be make-believe
      If you believed in me!"[29]

STELLA. What about the – Flamingo?

20 STANLEY. She stayed there, too.

STELLA. My sister lived at Belle Reve.

STANLEY. This is after the home-place had slipped through her lily-white fingers! She moved to the Flamingo! A second-class hotel which has the advan-

25 tage of not interfering in the private social life of the

---

1 **squeamishness:** Zimperlichkeit.
2 **line** (slang): hier: glattes Gerede.
4 **lily:** Lilie (Symbol der Unschuld, Jungfräulichkeit und Zerbrechlichkeit).
7 **supply-man:** Nachschubhalter, Materialeinkäufer.
14 **blithely** (adv.): munter, unbeschwert.
15f. **cardboard:** Pappe.
17 **make-believe:** Schein, (bloße) Phantasie.

personalities there! The Flamingo is used to all kinds
of goings-on. But even the management of the
Flamingo was impressed by Dame Blanche! In fact
they were so impressed by Dame Blanche that they
5   requested her to turn in her room-key – for perma-
nently! This happened a couple of weeks before she
showed here.

BLANCHE *(singing)*.

"It's a Barnum and Bailey world,
10   Just as phony as it can be –
But it wouldn't be make-believe
If you believed in me!"

STELLA. What – contemptible – lies!

STANLEY. Sure, I can see how you would be upset by this.
15   She pulled the wool over your eyes as much as Mitch's!

STELLA. It's pure invention! There's not a word of truth in
it and if I were a man and this creature had dared to
invent such things in my presence —

BLANCHE *(singing)*.

20   "Without your love,
It's a honky-tonk parade!
Without your love,
It's a melody played
In a penny arcade. . ."

25   STANLEY. Honey, I told you I thoroughly checked on

---

1 **personality** (iron.): Persönlichkeit.
2 **goings-on** (infml.): Dinge.
3 **Dame:** Dame (von Stand).
5 **to turn in:** hier: abgeben.
7 **to show** (infml.): sich blicken lassen, aufkreuzen.
9 **Barnum and Bailey:** Name eines berühmten amerikanischen Zirkus.
10 **phony:** unecht, gefälscht.
21 **honky-tonk** (AE, slang): (Nacht-)Schuppen, Bumslokal.
24 **penny arcade:** Spielhalle.

talking her round

these stories! Now wait till I finished. The trouble with
Dame Blanche was that she couldn't put on her act any
more in Laurel! They got wised up after two or three
dates with her and then they quit, and she goes on to
5 another, the same old lines, same old act, some old
hooey! But the town was too small for this to go on
forever! And as time went by she became a town
character. Regarded as not just different but downright loco – nuts.
10 *(Stella draws back.)*
And for the last year or two she has been washed up
like poison. That's why she's here this summer, visiting royalty, putting on all this act – because she's practically told by the mayor to get out of town! Yes, did
15 you know there was an army camp near Laurel and
your sister's was one of the places called "Out-of-
Bounds"?
BLANCHE.
    "It's only a paper moon,
20   Just as phony as it can be –
    But it wouldn't be make-believe
    If you believed in me!"
STANLEY. Well, so much for her being such a refined and

---

2 **to put on an act:** eine Schau abziehen.
3 **to get wised up:** hinter etwas kommen.
6 **hooey** (AE, slang): Gelaber.
7f. **town character:** etwa: stadtbekannte Person.
8f. **downright** (adv.): geradezu, glatt, ausgesprochen.
9 **loco** (AE, slang): bekloppt.
   nuts (infml.): durchgedreht.
11 **to be washed up:** am Ende sein.
13 **royalty:** königliche Familie; Mitglied der königlichen Familie.
14 **mayor:** Bürgermeister; hier: Stadtdirektor.
23 **refined:** fein.

particular type of girl. Which brings us to Lie Number
Two.

STELLA. I don't want to hear any more!

STANLEY. She's not going back to teach school! In fact I
am willing to bet you that she never had no idea of
returning to Laurel! She didn't resign temporarily
from the high school because of her nerves! No, siree,
Bob! She didn't. They kicked her out of that high
school before the spring term ended – and I hate to tell
you the reason that step was taken! A seventeen-year-
old boy – she'd gotten mixed up with!

stanley is a hypocrite

BLANCHE.

"It's a Barnum and Bailey world,
Just as phony as it can be — "

*(In the bathroom the water goes on loud; little breath-
less cries and peals of laughter are heard as if a child
were frolicking in the tub.)*

STELLA. This is making me – sick!

STANLEY. The boy's dad learned about it and got in touch
with the high school superintendent. Boy, oh, boy, I'd
like to have been in that office when Dame Blanche
was called on the carpet! I'd like to have seen her
trying to squirm out of that one! But they had her on
the hook good and proper that time and she knew that
the jig was all up! They told her she better move on to
some fresh territory. Yep, it was practickly a town
ordinance passed against her!

7f. **No, siree, Bob!** (AE, slang): Ganz bestimmt nicht!
17 **to frolic**: scherzen.
22 **to call s.o. on the carpet**: jdn. zur Minna machen.
23 **to squirm**: sich winden.
25 **the jig was all up**: das Spiel war endgültig aus.
26 **practickly** (adv.): *practically*.
26f. **town ordinance**: städtische Verordnung.

(The bathroom door is opened and Blanche thrusts her head out holding a towel about her hair.)

BLANCHE. Stella!

STELLA *(faintly)*. Yes, Blanche?

5 BLANCHE. Give me another bath-towel to dry my hair with. I've just washed it.

STELLA. Yes, Blanche. *(She crosses in a dazed way from the kitchen to the bathroom door with a towel.)*

BLANCHE. What's the matter, honey?

10 STELLA. Matter? Why?

BLANCHE. You have such a strange expression on your face!

STELLA. Oh — *(She tries to laugh.)* I guess I'm a little tired!

15 BLANCHE. Why don't you bathe, too, soon as I get out?

STANLEY *(calling from the kitchen)*. How soon is that going to be?

BLANCHE. Not so terribly long! Possess your soul in patience!

20 STANLEY. It's not my soul I'm worried about!

(Blanche slams the door. Stanley laughs harshly. Stella comes slowly back into the kitchen.)

STANLEY. Well, what do you think of it?

STELLA. I don't believe all of those stories and I think your

25 supply-man was mean and rotten to tell them. It's possible that some of the things he said are partly true. There are things about my sister I don't approve of – things that caused sorrow at home. She was always – flighty!

---

1 f. **to thrust out:** herausstrecken.
18 f. **to possess one's soul in patience:** sich in Geduld fassen.
21 **harshly** (adv.): rauh.
29 **flighty:** flatterhaft, gedankenlos.

STANLEY. Flighty is some word for it!

STELLA. But when she was young, very young, she had an experience that – killed her illusions!

STANLEY. What experience was that?

5 STELLA. I mean her marriage, when she was – almost a child! She married a boy who wrote poetry. . . . He was extremely good-looking. I think Blanche didn't just love him but worshipped the ground he walked on! Adored him and thought him almost too fine to be

10 human! But then she found out —

STANLEY. What?

STELLA. This beautiful and talented young man was a degenerate. Didn't your supply-man give you that information?

15 STANLEY. All we discussed was recent history. That must have been a pretty long time ago.

STELLA. Yes, it was – a pretty long time ago. . . .
(Stanley comes up and takes her by the shoulders rather gently. She gently withdraws from him. Automatically
20 *she starts sticking little pink candles in the birthday cake.)*

STANLEY. How many candles you putting in that cake?

STELLA. I'll stop at twenty-five.

STANLEY. Is company expected?

25 STELLA. We asked Mitch to come over for cake and ice-cream.
(Stanley looks a little uncomfortable. He lights a cigarette from the one he has just finished.)

STANLEY. I wouldn't be expecting Mitch over tonight.

---

12 **talented:** talentiert, begabt.
13 **degenerate:** degeneriert, entartet.
24 **company:** hier: Besuch.

*(Stella pauses in her occupation with candles and looks
slowly around at Stanley.)*

STELLA. Why?   [handwritten: band of brothers]

STANLEY. Mitch is a buddy of mine. We were in the same
5   outfit together – Two-forty-first Engineers. We work
in the same plant and now on the same bowling team.
You think I could face him if —

STELLA. Stanley Kowalski, did you – did you repeat what
that —?

10 STANLEY. You're goddam right I told him! I'd have that
on my conscience the rest of my life if I knew all that
stuff and let my best friend get caught!

STELLA. Is Mitch through with her?

STANLEY. Wouldn't you be if —?

15 STELLA. I said, *Is Mitch through with her?*

*(Blanche's voice is lifted again, serenely as a bell. She
sings*

"But it wouldn't be make-believe
If you believed in me.")

20 STANLEY. No, I don't think he's necessarily through with
her – just wised up!   [handwritten: sex but no marriage]

STELLA. Stanley, she thought Mitch was – going to – going
to marry her. I was hoping so, too.

STANLEY. Well, he's not going to marry her. Maybe he
25   *was*, but he's not going to jump in a tank with a school
of sharks – now! *(He rises.)* Blanche! Oh, Blanche!
Can I please get in my bathroom? *(There is a pause.)*

---

4 **buddy** (infml.): Kumpel.
5 **outfit**: Einheit, Truppe.
10 **goddam** (infml.): gottverdammt.
13 **to be through with s.o.:** mit jdm. fertig sein.
25 **tank:** *water-tank:* Wassertank, -behälter, -speicher.
25 f. **school of sharks:** Schwarm Haie.

BLANCHE. Yes, indeed, sir! Can you wait one second while I dry?

STANLEY. Having waited one hour I guess one second ought to pass in a hurry.

5 STELLA. And she hasn't got her job? Well, what will she do!

STANLEY. She's not stayin' here after Tuesday. You know that, don't you? Just to make sure I bought her ticket myself. A bus-ticket!

10 STELLA. In the first place, Blanche wouldn't go on a bus.

STANLEY. She'll go on a bus and like it.

STELLA. No, she won't, no, she won't, Stanley!

STANLEY. *She'll go!* Period. P.S. She'll go *Tuesday*!

STELLA *(slowly)*. What'll – she – do? What on earth will
15   she – *do*!

STANLEY. Her future is mapped out for her.

STELLA. What do you mean?
    (Blanche sings.)

STANLEY. Hey, canary bird! Toots! Get *OUT* of the
20   *BATHROOM*! Must I speak more plainly?
    *(The bathroom door flies open and Blanche emerges
    with a gay peal of laughter, but as Stanley crosses past
    her, a frightened look appears in her face, almost a look
    of panic. He doesn't look at her but slams the bathroom*
25   *door shut as he goes in.)*

BLANCHE *(snatching up a hair-brush)*. Oh, I feel so good after my long, hot bath, I feel so good and cool and – rested!

---

13 **period:** Punkt, Schluß.
16 **to be mapped out for s.o.:** für jdn. festgelegt, vorgezeichnet sein.
19 **toots** (infml.): Schätzchen.
21 **to emerge:** auftauchen.

STELLA *(sadly and doubtfully from the kitchen).* Do you,
Blanche?

BLANCHE *(brushing her hair vigorously).* Yes, I do, so
refreshed. *(She tinkles her highball glass.)* A hot bath
5 and a long, cold drink always gives me a brand new
outlook on life! *(She looks through the portières at
Stella, standing between them, and slowly stops brushing.)* Something has happened! – What is it?

STELLA *(turning quickly away).* Why, nothing has hap-
10 pened, Blanche.

BLANCHE. You're lying! Something has!

*(She stares fearfully at Stella, who pretends to be busy at
the table. The distant piano goes into a hectic break-
down.)*

---

3 **vigorously** (adv.): kräftig.
4 **to tinkle s.th.:** mit etwas klingeln, klimpern.
  highball: Longdrink aus Whisky, zerkleinertem Eis, Zitronenschale
  u. a.

Scene Eight

Three-quarters of an hour later.
The view through the big windows is fading gradually into
a still-golden dusk. A torch of sunlight blazes on the side
of a big water-tank or oil-drum across the empty lot
toward the business district which is now pierced by
pin-points of lighted windows or windows reflecting the
sunset.
The three people are completing a dismal birthday supper.
Stanley looks sullen. Stella is embarrassed and sad.
Blanche has a tight, artificial smile on her drawn face.
There is a fourth place at the table which is left vacant.

BLANCHE *(suddenly).* Stanley, tell us a joke, tell us a
funny story to make us all laugh. I don't know what's
the matter, we're all so solemn. Is it because I've been
stood up by my beau?
(Stella laughs feebly.)

---

4 **still-golden:** noch golden.
  torch: Fackel.
5 **oil-drum:** (zylindrischer) Ölbehälter.
  lot: Grundstück.
6 **business district:** Geschäftsviertel von New Orleans, südlich der Altstadt am Mississippi gelegen (s. Skizze).
7 **pin-point:** Punkt, Nadelkopf.
10 **sullen:** mürrisch.
12 **vacant:** unbesetzt, frei.
16 **to stand s.o. up** (infml.): jdn. ‚versetzen‘.
  beau: Kavalier.

It's the first time in my entire experience with men, and I've had a good deal of all sorts, that I've actually been stood up by anybody! Ha-ha! I don't know how to take it. . . . Tell us a funny little story, Stanley!
5 Something to help us out.

STANLEY. I didn't think you liked my stories, Blanche.

BLANCHE. I like them when they're amusing but not indecent.

STANLEY. I don't know any refined enough for your taste.

10 BLANCHE. Then let me tell one.

STELLA. Yes, you tell one, Blanche. You used to know lots of good stories.

(The music fades.)

BLANCHE. Let me see, now. . . . I must run through my
15 repertoire! Oh, yes – I love parrot stories! Do you all like parrot stories? Well, this one's about the old maid and the parrot. This old maid, she had a parrot that cursed a blue streak and knew more vulgar expressions than Mr. Kowalski!

20 STANLEY. Huh.

BLANCHE. And the only way to hush the parrot up was to put the cover back on its cage so it would think it was night and go back to sleep. Well, one morning the old maid had just uncovered the parrot for the day – when
25 who should she see coming up the front walk but the preacher! Well, she rushed back to the parrot and slipped the cover back on the cage and then she let in the preacher. And the parrot was perfectly still, just as

---

15 **parrot:** Papagei.
18 **to curse a blue streak:** am laufenden Band unanständig fluchen.
25 **front walk:** Weg zum Haus (von der Straßenseite).
26 **preacher:** Prediger.

quiet as a mouse, but just as she was asking the preacher how much sugar he wanted in his coffee – the parrot broke the silence with a loud – *(she whistles)* – and said – "God *damn*, but that was a short day!" truth shows

(She throws back her head and laughs. Stella also makes an ineffectual effort to seem amused. Stanley pays no attention to the story but reaches way over the table to spear his fork into the remaining chop which he eats with his fingers.)

BLANCHE. Apparently Mr. Kowalski was not amused.

STELLA. Mr. Kowalski is too busy making a pig of himself to think of anything else!

STANLEY. That's right, baby.

STELLA. Your face and your fingers are disgustingly greasy. Go and wash up and then help me clear the table.

(He hurls a plate to the floor.) destructive

STANLEY. That's how I'll clear the table! *(He seizes her arm.)* Don't ever talk that way to me! "Pig – Polack – disgusting – vulgar – greasy!" – them kind of words have been on your tongue and your sister's too much around here! What do you two think you are? A pair of queens? Remember what Huey Long[30] said – "Every Man is a King!" And I am the king around here, so don't forget it! *(He hurls a cup and saucer to the floor.)* My place is cleared! You want me to clear your places?

---

  7 **ineffectual:** unwirksam.
  9 **to spear:** bohren, stechen.
     chop: Kotelett.
 12 **to make a pig of o.s.** (slang): sich den Bauch vollschlagen.
 16 **greasy:** schmierig.
 26 **saucer:** Untertasse.

*(Stella begins to cry weakly. Stanley stalks out on the
porch and lights a cigarette.*

The Negro entertainers around the corner are heard.)

BLANCHE. What happened while I was bathing? What did
he tell you, Stella?

STELLA. Nothing, nothing, nothing!

BLANCHE. I think he told you something about Mitch and
me! You know why Mitch didn't come but you won't
tell me! *(Stella shakes her head helplessly.)* I'm going to
call him!

STELLA. I wouldn't call him, Blanche.

BLANCHE. I am, I'm going to call him on the phone.

STELLA *(miserably)*. I wish you wouldn't.

BLANCHE. I intend to be given some explanation from
someone!

*(She rushes to the phone in the bedroom. Stella goes out
on the porch and stares reproachfully at her husband.
He grunts and turns away from her.)*

STELLA. I hope you're pleased with your doings. I never
had so much trouble swallowing food in my life, looking at the girl's face and the empty chair. *(She cries
quietly.)*

BLANCHE *(at the phone)*. Hello. Mr. Mitchell, please. . . .
Oh. . . . I would like to leave a number if I may. Magnolia 9047. And say it's important to call. . . . Yes, very
important. . . . Thank you. *(She remains by the phone
with a lost, frightened look.)*

*(Stanley turns slowly back towards his wife and takes
her clumsily in his arms.)*

---

24 f. **Magnolia 9047:** Früher bestanden Telefonnummern aus Buchsta-
ben-Zahlen- oder Wort-Zahlen-Kombinationen. Die Magnolie ist
die Staats-Blume von Louisiana.

STANLEY. Stell, it's gonna be all right after she goes and
after you've had the baby. It's gonna be all right again
between you and me the way that it was. You
remember that way that it was? Them nights we had
5   together? God, honey, it's gonna be sweet when we
can make noise in the night the way that we used to and
get the coloured lights going with nobody's sister
behind the curtains to hear us!   *sex*
(Their upstairs neighbours are heard in bellowing
10   *laughter at something. Stanley chuckles.)*
Steve an' Eunice . . .

STELLA. Come on back in. *(She returns to the kitchen and
starts lighting the candles on the white cake.)* Blanche?

BLANCHE. Yes. *(She returns from the bedroom to the table
15   in the kitchen.)* Oh, those pretty, pretty little candles!
Oh, don't burn them, Stella.

STELLA. I certainly will.
(Stanley comes back in.)   *sugared*

BLANCHE. You ought to save them for baby's birthdays.
20   Oh, I hope candles are going to glow in his life and I
hope that his eyes are going to be like candles, like two
blue candles lighted in a white cake!

STANLEY *(sitting down)*. What poetry!

BLANCHE. His Auntie knows candles aren't safe, that can-
25   dles burn out in little boys' and girls' eyes, or wind
blows them out and after that happens, electric light
bulbs go on and you see too plainly . . . *(She pauses
reflectively for a moment.)* I shouldn't have called him.

---

7 **to get the coloured lights going:** hier (fig.): die farbigen Lampen
anzünden, ein Feuer anzünden.
10 **to chuckle:** kichern.
28 **reflectively** (adv.): nachdenklich.

STELLA. There's lots of things could have happened.

BLANCHE. There's no excuse for it, Stella. I don't have to put up with insults. I won't be taken for granted.

STANLEY. Goddamn, it's hot in here with the steam from the bathroom.

BLANCHE. I've said I was sorry three times. *(The piano fades out.)* I take hot baths for my nerves. Hydrotherapy, they call it. You healthy Polack, without a nerve in your body, of course you don't know what anxiety feels like!

STANLEY. I am not a Polack. People from Poland are Poles, not Polacks. But what I am is a one hundred per cent American, born and raised in the greatest country on earth and proud as hell of it, so don't ever call me a Polack.

(The phone rings. Blanche rises expectantly.)

BLANCHE. Oh, that's for me, I'm sure.

STANLEY. *I'm* not sure. Keep your seat. *(He crosses leisurely to phone.)* H'lo. Aw, yeh, hello, Mac.

(He leans against wall, staring insultingly in at Blanche. She sinks back in her chair with a frightened look. Stella leans over and touches her shoulder.)

BLANCHE. Oh, keep your hands off me, Stella. What is the matter with you? Why do you look at me with that pitying look?

STANLEY *(bawling)*. QUIET IN THERE! – We've got a noisy woman on the place. – Go on, Mac. At Riley's? No, I don't wanta bowl at Riley's. I had a little trouble with Riley last week. I'm the team-captain, ain't I? All right, then, we're not gonna bowl at Riley's, we're

---

3 **to take for granted:** als selbstverständlich ansehen.

7 f. **hydro-therapy:** Hydrotherapie, Wasserbehandlung.

gonna bowl at the West Side or the Gala! All right,
Mac. See you!
*(He hangs up and returns to the table. Blanche fiercely
controls herself, drinking quietly from her tumbler of*
5 *water. He doesn't look at her but reaches in a pocket.
Then he speaks slowly and with false amiability.)*
Sister Blanche, I've got a little birthday remembrance
for you. ~~sarcasm~~

BLANCHE. Oh, have you, Stanley? I wasn't expecting any,
10 I – I don't know why Stella wants to observe my birthday! I'd much rather forget it – when you – reach
twenty-seven! Well – age is a subject that you'd prefer
to – ignore!

STANLEY. Twenty-seven?

15 BLANCHE *(quickly)*. What is it? Is it for *me*?
(He is holding a little envelope towards her.)

STANLEY. Yes, I hope you like it!

BLANCHE. Why, why — Why, it's a —

STANLEY. Ticket! Back to Laurel! On the Greyhound!
20 Tuesday!
*(The Varsouviana music steals in softly and continues
playing. Stella rises abruptly and turns her back.
Blanche tries to smile. Then she tries to laugh. Then she
gives both up and springs from the table and runs in-*
25 *to the next room. She clutches her throat and then
runs into the bathroom. Coughing, gagging sounds are
heard.)*
Well!

STELLA. You didn't need to do that.

---

6 **amiability:** Liebenswürdigkeit.
19 **Greyhound:** Linie von Überlandbussen in den USA.
26 **to gag:** würgen (AE).

STANLEY. Don't forget all that I took off her.

STELLA. You needn't have been so cruel to someone alone as she is.

STANLEY. Delicate piece she is.

5 STELLA. She is. She was. You didn't know Blanche as a girl. Nobody, nobody, was tender and trusting as she was. But people like you abused her, and forced her to change.

(He crosses into the bedroom, ripping off his shirt, and
10 *changes into a brilliant silk bowling shirt. She follows him.)*

Do you think you're going bowling now?

STANLEY. Sure.

STELLA. You're not going bowling. *(She catches hold of*
15 *his shirt.)* Why did you do this to her?

STANLEY. I done nothing to no one. Let go of my shirt. You've torn it.

STELLA. I want to know why. Tell me why.

STANLEY. When we first met, me and you, you thought I
20 was common. How right you was, baby. I was common as dirt. You showed me the snapshot of the place with the columns. I pulled you down off them columns and how you loved it, having them coloured lights going! And wasn't we happy together, wasn't it all okay till
25 she showed here?

(Stella makes a slight movement. Her look goes sud-
denly inward as if some interior voice had called her
name. She begins a slow, shuffling progress from the
bedroom to the kitchen, leaning and resting on the back
30 *of the chair and then on the edge of a table with a blind*

---

7 **to abuse:** mißbrauchen, hintergehen.
27 **inward:** nach innen gerichtet.

*look and listening expression. Stanley, finishing with
his shirt, is unaware of her reaction.)*

And wasn't we happy together? Wasn't it all okay? Till
she showed here. Hoity-toity, describing me as an ape.
(He suddenly notices the change in Stella.) Hey, what is
it, Stel? *(He crosses to her.)*

STELLA *(quietly)*. Take me to the hospital.

*(He is with her now, supporting her with his arm, mur-
muring indistinguishably as they go outside. The "Varsouviana" is heard, its music rising with sinister rapidity
as the bathroom door opens slightly. Blanche comes
out twisting a washcloth. She begins to whisper the
words as the light fades slowly.)*

BLANCHE.

> *El pan de mais, el pan de mais,*
> *El pan de mais sin sal.*
> *El pan de mais, el pan de mais,*
> *El pan de mais sin sal . . .*

---

4 **hoity-toity** (infml.): hochnäsig, eingebildet.
8 **to be with s.o.:** jdn. verstehen.
10 **sinister:** unheilvoll.
   rapidity: Schnelligkeit.
12 **washcloth:** Waschlappen.
15 **El pan de mais** (richtig: *maíz*) **. . . sin sal** (Span.): Maisbrot . . . ohne
   Salz.

Scene Nine

A while later that evening. Blanche is seated in a tense hunched position in a bedroom chair that she has re-covered with diagonal green and white stripes. She has on
5 *her scarlet satin robe. On the table beside chair is a bottle of liquor and a glass. The rapid, feverish polka tune, the "Varsouviana," is heard. The music is in her mind; she is drinking to escape it and the sense of disaster clos-ing in on her, and she seems to whisper the words of the*
10 *song. An electric fan is turning back and forth across her.*

Mitch comes around the corner in work clothes: blue denim shirt and pants. He is unshaven. He climbs the steps to the door and rings. Blanche is startled.

15 BLANCHE. Who is it, please?
MITCH *(hoarsely)*. Me. Mitch.
   (The polka tune stops.)
BLANCHE. Mitch! – Just a minute.
   (She rushes about frantically, hiding the bottle in a
20   *closet, crouching at the mirror and dabbing her face with cologne and powder. She is so excited that her*

---

2 **tense:** gespannt.
4 **stripe:** Streifen.
8f. **to close in on s.o.:** sich über jdm. zusammenziehen.
10 **fan:** Ventilator.
19 **frantically** (adv.): wie wild geworden.
20 **to dab:** betupfen.

*breath is audible as she dashes about. At last she rushes
to the door in the kitchen and lets him in.)*

Mitch! – Y'know, I really shouldn't let you in after the
treatment I have received from you this evening! So
utterly uncavalier! But hello, beautiful!
*(She offers him her lips. He ignores it and pushes past
her into the flat. She looks fearfully after him as he
stalks into the bedroom.)*

My, my, what a cold shoulder! And a face like a thun-
dercloud! And such uncouth apparel! Why, you
haven't even shaved! The unforgivable insult to a lady!
But I forgive you. I forgive you because it's such a
relief to see you. You've stopped that polka tune that I
had caught in my head. Have you ever had anything
caught in your head? Some words, a piece of music?
That goes relentlessly on and on in your head? No, of
course you haven't, you dumb angel-puss, you'd never
get anything awful caught in your head!
*(He stares at her while he follows him while she talks. It
is obvious that he has had a few drinks on the way over.)*

MITCH. Do we have to have that fan on?

BLANCHE. No!

MITCH. I don't like fans.

BLANCHE. Then let's turn it off, honey. I'm not partial to
them!

---

1 **audible:** hörbar.
  to dash about: herumeilen.
5 **uncavalier:** wenig ritterlich, nicht wie ein Kavalier.
10 **uncouth:** ordinär, unfein.
  apparel: Kleidung.
14 **to catch:** hier: (genau) hören.
16 **relentlessly** (adv.): unbarmherzig.
17 **angel-puss** (slang): Engelsgesicht.
24 **to be partial to s.th.:** eine Schwäche für etwas haben.

(She presses the switch and the fan nods slowly off. She clears her throat uneasily as Mitch plumps himself down on the bed in the bedroom and lights a cigarette.)
I don't know what there is to drink. I – haven't investi-
5 gated.

MITCH. I don't want Stan's liquor.

BLANCHE. It isn't Stan's. Everything here isn't Stan's. Some things on the premises are actually mine! How is your mother? Isn't your mother well?

10 MITCH. Why?

BLANCHE. Something's the matter tonight, but never mind. I won't cross-examine the witness. I'll just *(She touches her forehead vaguely. The polka tune starts up again.)* – pretend I don't notice anything dif-
15 ferent about you! That – music again . . .

MITCH. What music?

BLANCHE. The "Varsouviana"! The polka tune they were playing when Allan — Wait!
*(A distant revolver shot is heard. Blanche seems re-
20 lieved.)*
There now, the shot! It always stops after that.
(The polka music dies out again.)
Yes, now it's stopped.

MITCH. Are you boxed out of your mind?

25 BLANCHE. I'll go and see what I can find in the way of — *(She crosses into the closet, pretending to search for the bottle.)* Oh, by the way, excuse me for not being

---

1 **to nod off:** eigtl.: einnicken; hier: aufhören, sich zu drehen.
2 **to plump o.s.:** sich fallen lassen.
8 **on the premises** (pl.): in diesem Hause.
12 **to cross-examine:** ins Kreuzverhör nehmen.
24 **to be boxed out of one's mind:** etwa: nicht ganz bei Trost sein.

dressed! But I'd practically given you up! Had you
forgotten your invitation to supper?

MITCH. I wasn't going to see you any more.

BLANCHE. Wait a minute. I can't hear what you're saying
5   and you talk so little that when you do say something, I
don't want to miss a single syllable of it. . . . What am I
looking around here for? Oh, yes – liquor! We've had
so much excitement around here this evening that I *am*
boxed out of my mind! *(She pretends suddenly to find*
10   *the bottle. He draws his foot up on the bed and stares*
at her contemptuously.) Here's something. Southern
Comfort! What is that, I wonder?

MITCH. If you don't know, it must belong to Stan.

BLANCHE. Take your foot off the bed. It has a light cover
15   on it. Of course you boys don't notice things like that.
I've done so much with this place since I've been here.

MITCH. I bet you have.

BLANCHE. You saw it before I came. Well, look at it now!
This room is almost – dainty! I want to keep it that
20   way. I wonder if this stuff ought to be mixed with
something? Ummm, it's sweet, so sweet! It's terribly,
terribly sweet! Why, it's a *liqueur*, I believe! Yes,
that's what it *is*, a liqueur! *(Mitch grunts.)* I'm afraid
you won't like it, but try it, and maybe you will.

25   MITCH. I told you already I don't want none of his liquor
and I mean it. You ought to lay off his liquor. He says
you been lapping it up all summer like a wild-cat!

BLANCHE. What a fantastic statement! Fantastic of him to

---

11 f. **Southern Comfort:** »Matthew's Southern Comfort«, Name eines
berühmten amerikanischen Whiskey-Likörs.

22 **liqueur:** Likör.

28 **fantastic:** unglaublich, aus der Luft gegriffen.

say it, fantastic of you to repeat it! I won't descend to the level of such cheap accusations to answer them, even!

MITCH. Huh.

5 BLANCHE. What's in your mind? I see something in your eyes!

MITCH *(getting up)*. It's dark in here.

BLANCHE. I like it dark. The dark is comforting to me.

MITCH. I don't think I ever seen you in the light. *(Blanche*
0 *laughs breathlessly.)* That's a fact!

BLANCHE. Is it?

MITCH. I've never seen you in the afternoon.

BLANCHE. Whose fault is that?

MITCH. You never want to go out in the afternoon.

5 BLANCHE. Why, Mitch, you're at the plant in the afternoon!

MITCH. Not Sunday afternoon. I've asked you to go out with me sometimes on Sundays but you always make an excuse. You never want to go out till after six and
0 then it's always some place that's not lighted much.

BLANCHE. There is some obscure meaning in this but I fail to catch it.

MITCH. What it means is I've never had a real good look at you, Blanche.

5 BLANCHE. What are you leading up to?

MITCH. Let's turn the light on here.

BLANCHE *(fearfully)*. Light? Which light? What for?

MITCH. This one with the paper thing on it. *(He tears the paper lantern off the light bulb. She utters a frightened*
0 *gasp.)*

---

21 **obscure:** dunkel, verborgen.
25 **to lead up to s.th.:** auf etwas hinauswollen.
30 **gasp:** schwerer Atemzug.

BLANCHE. What did you do that for?

MITCH. So I can take a look at you good and plain!

BLANCHE. Of course you don't really mean to be insulting!

5 MITCH. No, just realistic.

BLANCHE. I don't want realism.

MITCH. Naw, I guess not.

BLANCHE. I'll tell you what I want. Magic! *(Mitch laughs.)*
Yes, yes, magic! I try to give that to people. I misrepre-
10 sent things to them. I don't tell truth, I tell what *ought*
to be truth. And if that is sinful, then let me be damned
for it! – *Don't turn the light on!*
*(Mitch crosses to the switch. He turns the light on and
stares at her. She cries out and covers her face. He turns*
15 *the light off again.)*

MITCH *(slowly and bitterly)*. I don't mind you being older
than what I thought. But all the rest of it – God! That
pitch about your ideals being so old-fashioned and all
the malarkey that you've dished out all summer. Oh, I
20 knew you weren't sixteen any more. But I was a fool
enough to believe you was straight.

BLANCHE. Who told you I wasn't – "straight"! My loving
brother-in-law. And you believed him.

MITCH. I called him a liar at first. And then I checked on
25 the story. First I asked our supply-man who travels
through Laurel. And then I talked directly over long-
distance to this merchant.

BLANCHE. Who is the merchant?

---

9 f. **to misrepresent:** falsch darstellen.
17 f. **that pitch about . . .** (AE, slang): das mit . . .
19 **malarkey** (infml.): Hokuspokus.
   to dish out: auftischen, austeilen.
26 f. **to talk over long-distance:** ein Ferngespräch führen.

MITCH. Kiefaber.

BLANCHE. The merchant Kiefaber of Laurel! I know the man. He whistled at me. I put him in his place. So now for revenge he makes up stories about me.

5 MITCH. Three people, Kiefaber, Stanley and Shaw, swore to them!

BLANCHE. Rub-a-dub-dub, three men in a tub! And such a filthy tub!

MITCH. Didn't you stay at a hotel called The Flamingo?

10 BLANCHE. Flamingo? No! Tarantula was the name of it! I stayed at a hotel called The Tarantula Arms!

MITCH (*stupidly*). Tarantula?

BLANCHE. Yes, a big spider! That's where I brought my victims. (*She pours herself another drink.*) Yes, I had

15 many intimacies with strangers. After the death of Allan – intimacies with strangers was all I seemed able to fill my empty heart with. . . . I think it was panic, just panic, that drove me from one to another, hunting for some protection – here and

20 there, in the most – unlikely places – even, at last, in a seventeen-year-old boy but – somebody wrote the superintendent about it – "This woman is morally unfit for her position!"

---

3 **to put s.o. in his, her place:** es jdm. zeigen, jdn. zum Schweigen bringen.

7 **rub-a-dub-dub:** etwa: rubbel-rubbel (Anfang eines Kinderreims aus dem Jahr 1798).
  tub: Faß, Tonne, Zuber.

10 **Tarantula:** Tarantel.

11 **arms** (pl.): Wappen.

13 **spider:** Spinne.

15 **intimacy:** Intimität, Vertraulichkeit.

20 **unlikely:** unwahrscheinlich.

*(She throws back her head with convulsive, sobbing
laughter.
Then she repeats the statement, gasps, and drinks.)*
True? Yes, I suppose – unfit somehow – anyway. . . .
5   So I came here. There was nowhere else I could go. I
was played out. You know what played out is? My
youth was suddenly gone up the water-spout, and – I
met you. You said you needed somebody. Well, I
needed somebody, too. I thanked God for you, be-
10 cause you seemed to be gentle – a cleft in the rock of
the world that I could hide in! The poor man's Paradise
– is a little peace. . . . But I guess I was asking, hoping –
too much! Kiefaber, Stanley and Shaw have tied an old
tin can to the tail of the kite.
15 *(There is a pause. Mitch stares at her dumbly.)*
MITCH. You lied to me, Blanche.
BLANCHE. Don't say I lied to you.
MITCH. Lies, lies, inside and out, all lies.
BLANCHE. Never inside, I didn't lie in my heart. . . .
20 *(A Vendor comes around the corner. She is a blind
Mexican woman in a dark shawl, carrying bunches of
those gaudy tin flowers that lower class Mexicans dis-
play at funerals and other festive occasions. She is calling barely audibly. Her figure is only faintly visible
25 outside the building.)*
MEXICAN WOMAN. *Flores. Flores. Flores para los muertos.
Flores. Flores.*

---

6 **to be played out:** ausgespielt haben, verbraucht sein.
7 **to go up the water-spout** (fig.): sich in einem Wolkenbruch auflösen.
10 **cleft:** Spalte.
14 **kite:** hier: Person, die jdn. ausnutzt, Parasit.
21 **shawl:** Umhang, Umhängetuch; Kopftuch.
26 **flores para los muertos** (Span.): Blumen für die Toten.

BLANCHE. What? Oh! Somebody outside. . . . I – I lived in
a house where dying old women remembered their
dead men . . .

MEXICAN WOMAN. *Flores. Flores para los muertos* . . .
5 *(The polka tune fades in.)*

BLANCHE *(as if to herself)*. Crumble and fade and – regrets
– recriminations . . . "If you'd done this, it wouldn't've
cost me that!"

MEXICAN WOMAN. *Corones para los muertos. Corones* . . .

10 BLANCHE. Legacies! Huh. . . . And other things such as
blood-stained pillow-slips – "Her linen needs changing" – "Yes Mother. But couldn't we get a coloured
girl to do it?" No, we couldn't of course. Everything
gone but the —

15 MEXICAN WOMAN. *Flores.*

BLANCHE. Death – I used to sit here and she used to sit
over there and death was as close as you are. . . . We
didn't dare even admit we had ever heard of it!

MEXICAN WOMAN. *Flores para los muertos, flores –*
20 *flores* .

BLANCHE. The opposite is desire. So do you wonder?
How could you possibly wonder! Not far from Belle
Reve, before we had lost Belle Reve, was a camp
where they trained young soldiers. On Saturday nights
25 they would go in town to get drunk —

MEXICAN WOMAN *(softly)*. *Corones*. . . .

BLANCHE. – and on the way back they would stagger on to

---

5 **to fade in:** hier: eingeblendet werden.
6 **to crumble:** zerbröckeln.
7 **recrimination:** Vorwurf.
9 **corones** (Span.): Kränze, Kronen.
10 **legacy:** Erbschaft, Vermächtnis.
11 **pillow-slip:** Kopfkissenbezug.

my lawn and call – "Blanche! Blanche!" – The deaf old
lady remaining suspected nothing. But sometimes I
slipped outside to answer their calls. . . . Later the
paddy-wagon would gather them up like daisies . . .
5   the long way home . . .

*(The Mexican woman turns slowly and drifts back off
with her soft mournful cries. Blanche goes to the dresser
and leans forward on it. After a moment, Mitch rises
and follows her purposefully. The polka music fades*
10 *away. He places his hands on her waist and tries to turn
her about.)*

BLANCHE. What do you want?

MITCH *(fumbling to embrace her)*. What I been missing all
summer.

15 BLANCHE. Then marry me, Mitch!

MITCH. I don't think I want to marry you any more.

BLANCHE. No?

MITCH *(dropping his hands from her waist)*. You're not
clean enough to bring in the house with my mother.

20 BLANCHE. Go away, then. *(He stares at her.)* Get out of
here quick before I start screaming fire! *(Her throat is
tightening with hysteria.)* Get out of here quick before I
start screaming fire.

(He still remains staring. She suddenly rushes to the big
25 *window with its pale blue square of the soft summer
light and cries wildly.)*

Fire! Fire! Fire!

---

4 **paddy-wagon** (AE, slang): grüne Minna, Polizeiauto.
7 **mournful:** traurig.
9 **purposefully** (adv.): entschlossen.
21 f. **Her throat is tightening with hysteria:** Hysterie schnürt ihr die
    Kehle zusammen.

(*With a startled gasp, Mitch turns and goes out of the outer door, clatters awkwardly down the steps and around the corner of the building. Blanche staggers back from the window and falls to her knees. The distant piano is slow and blue.*)

Scene Ten

It is a few hours later that night.
Blanche has been drinking fairly steadily since Mitch left.
She has dragged her wardrobe trunk into the centre of the
5 *bedroom. It hangs open with flowery dresses thrown*
across it. As the drinking and packing went on, a mood of
hysterical exhilaration came into her and she has decked
herself out in a somewhat soiled and crumpled white satin
evening gown and a pair of scuffed silver slippers with
10 *brilliants set in their heels.*
Now she is placing the rhinestone tiara on her head before
the mirror of the dressing-table and murmuring excitedly
as if to a group of spectral admirers.

BLANCHE. How about taking a swim, a moonlight swim at
15 the old rock-quarry? If anyone's sober enough to drive
a car! Ha-Ha! Best way in the world to stop your head
buzzing! Only you've got to be careful to dive where
the deep pool is – if you hit a rock you don't come up
till tomorrow. . . .
20 *(Tremblingly she lifts the hand mirror for a closer*
inspection. She catches her breath and slams the mirror

---

7 **exhilaration:** Hochgefühl.
7 f. **to deck o.s. out:** sich ausstaffieren, sich schmücken.
8 **crumpled:** zerknittert.
9 **scuffed:** abgetragen.
   slippers: hier: Pumps, hochhackige Damenschuhe.
13 **spectral:** gespensterhaft.
15 **rock-quarry:** Steinbruch.

face down with such violence that the glass cracks. She
moans a little and attempts to rise.)
(Stanley appears around the corner of the building. He
still has on the vivid green silk bowling shirt. As he
5 *rounds the corner the honky-tonk music is heard. It*
continues softly throughout the scene.
He enters the kitchen, slamming the door. As he peers
in at Blanche, he gives a low whistle. He has had a few
drinks on the way and has brought some quart beer
10 *bottles home with him.)*

BLANCHE. How is my sister?

STANLEY. She is doing okay.

BLANCHE. And how is the baby?

STANLEY *(grinning amiably)*. The baby won't come be-
15 fore morning so they told me to go home and get a little
shut-eye.

BLANCHE. Does that mean we are to be alone in here?

STANLEY. Yep. Just me and you, Blanche. Unless you got
somebody hid under the bed. What've you got on
20 those fine feathers for?

BLANCHE. Oh, that's right. You left before my wire came.

STANLEY. You got a wire?

BLANCHE. I received a telegram from an old admirer of
mine.

25 STANLEY. Anything good?

BLANCHE. I think so. An invitation.

STANLEY. What to? A fireman's ball?

---

7 f. **to peer in:** hereinschauen.
9 **quart:** Viertelgallone (0,946 l USA).
14 **amiably** (adv.): liebenswürdig.
16 **shut-eye** (slang): Nickerchen.
27 **fireman's ball:** etwa: Pioniere-Ball; (*fireman:* US-Marinepionier für
allgemeine Aufgaben [AE]).

BLANCHE *(throwing back her head)*. A cruise of the Caribbean on a yacht!

STANLEY. Well, well. What do you know?

BLANCHE. I have never been so surprised in my life.

5 STANLEY. I guess not.

BLANCHE. It came like a bolt from the blue!

STANLEY. Who did you say it was from?

BLANCHE. An old beau of mine.

STANLEY. The one that give you the white fox-pieces?

10 BLANCHE. Mr. Shep Huntleigh. I wore his ATO pin my last year at college. I hadn't seen him again until last Christmas. I ran in to him on Biscayne Boulevard. Then – just now – this wire – inviting me on a cruise of the Caribbean! The problem is clothes. I tore into my

15 trunk to see what I have that's suitable for the tropics!

STANLEY. And come up with that – gorgeous – diamond – tiara?

BLANCHE. This old relic! Ha-ha! It's only rhinestones.

STANLEY. Gosh. I thought it was Tiffany diamonds. *(He*

20 *unbuttons his shirt.)*

BLANCHE. Well, anyhow, I shall be entertained in style.

STANLEY. Uh-huh. It goes to show, you never know what is coming.

---

1 **cruise:** Kreuzfahrt.

1 f. **Caribbean:** Karibik.

6 **bolt from the blue:** Blitz aus heiterem Himmel.

10 **ATO pin:** Anstecknadel einer »fraternity« (Studentenverbindung) mit dem Namen Alpha, Tau, Omega, dessen Bedeutung nur Eingeweihten bekannt ist.

14 **to tear into s.th.:** sich über etwas hermachen.

18 **relic:** Überbleibsel.

19 **Gosh** (infml.): Mensch!

   Tiffany: Name eines berühmten Juweliers in New York.

21 **in style** (adv.): stilvoll.

BLANCHE. Just when I thought my luck had begun to fail
me —

STANLEY. Into the picture pops this Miami millionaire.

BLANCHE. This man is not from Miami. This man is from
5   Dallas.

STANLEY. This man is from Dallas?

BLANCHE. Yes, this man is from Dallas where gold spouts
out of the ground!

STANLEY. Well, just so he's from somewhere! *(He starts
10   removing his shirt.)*

BLANCHE. Close the curtains before you undress any
further.

STANLEY *(amiably)*. This is all I'm going to undress right
now. *(He rips the sack off a quart beer-bottle.)* Seen a
15   bottle-opener?

*(She moves slowly towards the dresser, where she
stands with her hands knotted together.)*

I used to have a cousin who could open a beer-bottle
with his teeth. *(Pounding the bottle cap on the corner of*
20   *table.)* That was his only accomplishment, all he could
do – he was just a human bottle-opener. And then one
time, at a wedding party, he broke his front teeth off!
After that he was so ashamed of himself he used
t' sneak out of the house when company came . . .

25   *(The bottle cap pops off and a geyser of foam shoots up.*
Stanley laughs happily, holding up the bottle over his
head.)

---

14 **sack:** hier: Papiertüte (zum Einkaufen).
19 **to pound:** hämmern, fest schlagen.
20 **accomplishment:** Fertigkeit.
24 **to sneak:** schleichen.
25 **geyser:** Fontäne.

Ha-ha! Rain from heaven! *(He extends the bottle towards her.)* <u>Shall we bury the hatchet and make it a loving-cup?</u> Huh? *wants to make up*

BLANCHE. No, thank you.

5 STANLEY. Well, it's a red letter night for us both. You having an oil-millionaire and me having a baby.

(He goes to the bureau in the bedroom and crouches to remove something from the bottom drawer.)

BLANCHE *(drawing back)*. What are you doing in here?

10 STANLEY. Here's something I always break out on special occasions like this! The silk pyjamas I wore on my wedding night!

BLANCHE. Oh.

STANLEY. When the telephone rings and they say,
15 "You've got a son!" I'll tear this off and wave it like a flag! *(He shakes out a brilliant pyjama coat.)* I guess we are both entitled to put on the dog. *(He goes back to the kitchen with the coat over his arm.)*

BLANCHE. When I think of how divine it is going to be to
20 have such a thing as privacy once more – I could weep with joy!

STANLEY. This millionaire from Dallas is not going to interfere with your privacy any?

BLANCHE. It won't be the sort of thing you have in mind.
25 This man is a gentleman and he respects me. *(Improvising feverishly.)* What he wants is my companion-

---

1 **to extend:** hinhalten, anbieten.
2 **to bury the hatchet** (fig.): die Streitaxt begraben.
3 **loving-cup:** Pokal, hier: gemeinsames Trinkgefäß bei einer Feier.
5 **red letter night:** besonderer Abend.
17 **to put on the dog** (infml.): auf fein machen.
23 **any:** hier: überhaupt.
25 f. **to improvise:** improvisieren.

ship. Having great wealth sometimes makes people
lonely!

STANLEY. I wouldn't know about that.

BLANCHE. A cultivated woman, a woman of intelligence
5   and breeding, can enrich a man's life – immeasurably!
I have those things to offer, and this doesn't take them
away. Physical beauty is passing. A transitory posses-
sion. But beauty of the mind and richness of the spirit
and tenderness of the heart – and I have all of those
10   things – aren't taken away, but grow! Increase with the
years! How strange that I should be called a destitute
woman! When I have all of these treasures locked in
my heart. (*A choked sob comes from her.*) I think of
myself as a very, very rich woman! But I have been
15   foolish – casting my pearls before swine!

STANLEY. Swine, huh?

BLANCHE. Yes, swine! Swine! And I'm thinking not only
of you but of your friend, Mr. Mitchell. He came to see
me tonight. He dared to come here in his work-
20   clothes! And to repeat slander to me, vicious stories
that he had gotten from you! I gave him his walking
papers . . .

STANLEY. You did, huh?

BLANCHE. But then he came back. He returned with a box

---

5 **breeding:** Bildung.
   immeasurably (adv.). unschätzbar, unendlich.
7 **transitory:** vorübergehend.
11 **destitute:** mittellos, arm.
15 **to cast one's pearls before swine** (infml., fig.): (seine) Perlen vor die
   Säue werfen.
20 **slander:** Verleumdung.
   vicious: bösartig.
21 f. **walking papers:** Entlassungspapiere.

of roses to beg my forgiveness! He implored my forgiveness. But some things are not forgivable. Deliber-
ate cruelty is not forgivable. It is the one unforgivable
thing in my opinion and it is the one thing of which I
5   have never, never been guilty. And so I told him, I said
to him, "Thank you," but it was foolish of me to think
that we could ever adapt ourselves to each other. Our
ways of life are too different. Our attitudes and our
backgrounds are incompatible. We have to be realistic
10   about such things. So farewell, my friend! And let
there be no hard feelings . . .

STANLEY. Was this before or after the telegram came from
the Texas oil millionaire?

BLANCHE. What telegram? No! No, after! As a matter of
15   fact, the wire came just as —

STANLEY. As a matter of fact there wasn't no wire at
all!

BLANCHE. Oh, oh!

STANLEY. There isn't no millionaire! And Mitch didn't
20   come back with roses 'cause I know where he is —

BLANCHE. Oh!

STANLEY. There isn't a goddam thing but imagination!

BLANCHE. Oh!

STANLEY. And lies and conceit and tricks!

25   BLANCHE. Oh!

STANLEY. And look at yourself! Take a look at yourself in
that worn-out Mardi Gras outfit, rented for fifty cents

---

1 **to implore:** erflehen.
9 **incompatible:** unvereinbar.
24 **conceit:** Dünkel.
27 **Mardi Gras** (Fr.): Fastnacht; wörtl.: fetter Dienstag.
    outfit: hier: Aufmachung.

from some rag-picker! And with the crazy crown on!
What queen do you think you are!

BLANCHE. Oh – God . . .

STANLEY. I've been on to you from the start! Not once did
5 you pull any wool over this boy's eyes! You come in
here and sprinkle the place with powder and spray
perfume and cover the light-bulb with a paper lantern,
and lo and behold the place has turned into Egypt and
you are the Queen of the Nile! Sitting on your throne
10 and swilling down my liquor! I say – *Ha – Ha!* Do you
hear me? *Ha – ha – ha! (He walks into the bedroom.)*

BLANCHE. Don't come in here!

(Lurid reflections appear on the walls around Blanche.
The shadows are of a grotesque and menacing form.
15 *She catches her breath, crosses to the phone and jiggles*
the hook. Stanley goes into the bathroom and closes the
door.)

Operator, operator! Give me long-distance, please.
. . . I want to get in touch with Mr. Shep Huntleigh of
20 Dallas. He's so well-known he doesn't require any
address. Just ask anybody who Wait! No, I
couldn't find it right now. . . . Please understand, I –
No! No, wait! . . . One moment! Someone is –
Nothing! Hold on, please!

---

1 **rag-picker:** Lumpensammler.
4 **to be on to s.o.:** jdm. auf die Schliche kommen.
6 **to sprinkle:** besprühen.
8 **lo and behold** (poet.): und siehe da.
9 **Queen of the Nile:** Königin vom Nil; gemeint ist Cleopatra.
14 **grotesque:** grotesk, verzerrt, wunderlich.
   menacing: drohend.
15 **to jiggle s.th.:** an etwas rütteln.
16 **hook:** hier: Haken, an dem der Telefonhörer hängt.
19 **to get in touch with s.o.:** mit jdm. verbunden werden.

*(She sets the phone down and crosses warily into the
kitchen.
The night is filled with inhuman voices like cries in a
jungle.*
5   *The shadows and lurid reflections move sinuously as
flames along the wall spaces.
Through the back wall of the rooms, which have
become transparent, can be seen the sidewalk. A prostitute has rolled a drunkard. He pursues her along the*
10   *walk, overtakes her and there is a struggle. A police-
man's whistle breaks it up. The figures disappear.
Some moments later the Negro woman appears around
the corner with a sequined bag which the prostitute had
dropped on the walk. She is rooting excitedly through*
15   *it.
Blanche presses her knuckles to her lips and returns
slowly to the phone. She speaks in a hoarse whisper.)*
Operator! Operator! Never mind long-distance. Get
Western Union. There isn't time to be – Western –
20   Western Union!
(She waits anxiously.)
Western Union? Yes! I – want to – Take down this
message! "In desperate, desperate circumstances!
Help me! Caught in a trap. Caught in —" *Oh!*
25   *The bathroom door is thrown open and Stanley comes*

---

1 **warily** (adv.): vorsichtig.
5 **sinuously** (adv.): sich schlängelnd, in Bögen.
6 **wall spaces:** hier: Wände.
8 **transparent:** durchsichtig.
9 **to roll** (AE, slang): bestehlen (besonders im Zusammenhang mit Be-
    trunkenen).
10 **to overtake:** einholen.
13 **sequined:** mit Pailletten besetzt.

*out in the brilliant silk pyjamas. He grins at her as he
knots the tasselled sash about his waist. She gasps and
backs away from the phone. He stares at her for a count
of ten. Then a clicking becomes audible from the tele-*
5 *phone, steady and rasping.*

STANLEY. You left th' phone off th' hook.

*(He crosses to it deliberately and sets it back on the
hook. After he has replaced it, he stares at her again, his
mouth slowly curving into a grin, as he waves between*
10 *Blanche and the outer door.*

*The barely audible "blue piano" begins to drum up
louder. The sound of it turns into the roar of an
approaching locomotive. Blanche crouches, pressing
her fists to her ears until it has gone by.)*

15 BLANCHE *(finally straightening).* Let me – let me get by
you!

STANLEY. Get by me? Sure. Go ahead. *(He moves back a
pace in the doorway.)*

BLANCHE. You – you stand over there! *(She indicates a*
20 *further position.)*

STANLEY *(grinning).* You got plenty of room to walk by
me now.

BLANCHE. Not with you there! But I've got to get out
somehow! *putting ideas in his head?*

25 STANLEY. You think I'll interfere with you? Ha-ha!

*(The "blue piano" goes softly. She turns confusedly and
makes a faint gesture. The inhuman jungle voices rise*

---

2 **tasselled:** mit Quaste, mit Troddel.
  sash: Schärpe; hier: Gürtel.
4 **clicking:** Klicken, Knacken.
5 **rasping:** kratzend.
11 **to drum up:** hier: spielen (um die Aufmerksamkeit zu erregen).
15f. **to get by s.o.:** an jdm. vorbeigehen.

up. He takes a step towards her, biting his tongue which protrudes between his lips.)

STANLEY *(softly)*. Come to think of it – maybe you wouldn't be bad to – interfere with . . .

(Blanche moves backward through the door into the bedroom.)

BLANCHE. Stay back! Don't you come towards me another step or I'll —

STANLEY. What?

BLANCHE. Some awful thing will happen! It will!

STANLEY. What are you putting on now?

(They are now both inside the bedroom.)

BLANCHE. I warn you, don't, I'm in danger!

(He takes another step. She smashes a bottle on the table and faces him, clutching the broken top.)

STANLEY. What did you do that for?

BLANCHE. So I could twist the broken end in your face!

STANLEY. I bet you would do that!

BLANCHE. I would! I will if you —

STANLEY. Oh! So you want some rough-house! All right, let's have some rough-house!

(He springs towards her, overturning the table. She cries out and strikes at him with the bottle top but he catches her wrist.)

Tiger – tiger! Drop the bottle-top! Drop it! We've had this date with each other from the beginning!

(She moans. The bottle-tops falls. She sinks to her knees. He picks up her inert figure and carries her to the bed. The hot trumpet and drums from the Four Deuces sound loudly.)

---

2 **to protrude**: hervorstehen.
20 **rough-house**: Schlägerei.
28 **inert**: leblos.

Scene Eleven

It is some weeks later. Stella is packing Blanche's things.
Sound of water can be heard running in the bathroom.
The portières are partly open on the poker players – Stan-
5 *ley, Steve, Mitch and Pablo – who sit around the table in*
the kitchen. The atmosphere of the kitchen is now the same
raw, lurid one of the disastrous poker night.
The building is framed by the sky of turquoise. Stella has
been crying as she arranges the flowery dresses in the open
10 *trunk.*
Eunice comes down the steps from her flat above and
enters the kitchen. There is another burst from the poker
table.

STANLEY. Drew to an inside straight and made it, by God.
15 PABLO. *Maldita sea tu suerto!*
STANLEY. Put it in English, greaseball.
PABLO. I am cursing your goddam luck.
STANLEY *(prodigiously elated)*. You know what luck is?

---

7 **disastrous:** verheerend, katastrophal.
14 **to draw:** (Karte) ziehen.
   inside straight: vier Karten eines Pokerblatts, die durch Ziehen einer
   weiteren Karte zu einer »Straße« werden können (etwa 6, 7, 9, 10; die
   8 ergibt die Straße, unabhängig von der Farbe der einzelnen Karten).
15 **Maldita sea tu suerto** (Span.): Verflucht sei dein Glück.
16 **greaseball** (slang): etwa: Fettkloß (Schimpfwort für einen Mexi-
   kaner).
18 **prodigiously** (adv.): außerordentlich.
   elated: hochgestimmt.

Luck is believing you're lucky. Take at Salerno.[31] I
believed I was lucky. I figured that 4 out of 5 would not
come through but I would ... and I did. I put that
down as a rule. To hold front position in this rat-race
5 you've got to believe you are lucky.

MITCH. You ... you ... you. ... Brag ... brag ...
bull ... bull.

*(Stella goes into the bedroom and starts folding a
dress.)*

10 STANLEY. What's the matter with him?

EUNICE *(walking past the table)*. I always did say that men
are callous things with no feelings, but this does beat
anything. Making pigs of yourselves. *(She comes
through the portières into the bedroom.)*

15 STANLEY. What's the matter with her?

STELLA. How is my baby?

EUNICE. Sleeping like a little angel. Brought you some
grapes. *(She puts them on a stool and lowers her voice.)*
Blanche?

20 STELLA. Bathing.

EUNICE. How is she?

STELLA. She wouldn't eat anything but asked for a drink.

EUNICE. What did you tell her?

STELLA. I – just told her that – we'd made arrangements
25 for her to rest in the country. She's got it mixed in her
mind with Shep Huntleigh.

(Blanche opens the bathroom door slightly.)

BLANCHE. Stella.

---

4 **rat-race:** ständiger Konkurrenzkampf.
6 **to brag:** prahlen.
12 **callous:** gefühllos.
18 **stool:** Hocker, Schemel.

STELLA. Yes, Blanche?

BLANCHE. If anyone calls while I'm bathing take the number and tell them I'll call right back.

STELLA. Yes.

5 BLANCHE. That cool yellow silk – the bouclé. See if it's crushed. If it's not too crushed I'll wear it and on the lapel that silver and turquoise pin in the shape of a seahorse. You will find them in the heart-shaped box I keep my accessories in. And Stella . . . Try and locate a

10 bunch of artificial violets in that box, too, to pin with the seahorse on the lapel of the jacket.

(She closes the door. Stella turns to Eunice.)

STELLA. I don't know if I did the right thing.

EUNICE. What else could you do?

15 STELLA. I couldn't believe her story and go on living with Stanley.

EUNICE. Don't ever believe it. Life has got to go on. No matter what happens, you've got to keep on going.

(The bathroom door opens a little.)

20 BLANCHE *(looking out)*. Is the coast clear?

STELLA. Yes, Blanche. *(To Eunice.)* Tell her how well she's looking.

BLANCHE. Please close the curtains before I come out.

STELLA. They're closed.

25 STANLEY. – How many for you

PABLO. Two. –

STEVE. – Three.

5 **bouclé:** Bouclé (Stoff aus Garn mit Knoten und Schlingen).
6 **crushed:** zerknittert.
7 **lapel:** Revers, Jackenaufschlag.
9 **accessories:** Accessoires (wie etwa Modeschmuck).
10 **violet:** Veilchen.
20 **Is the coast clear?:** Ist die Luft rein?

(Blanche appears in the amber light of the door. She has a tragic radiance in her red satin robe following the sculptural lines of her body. The "Varsouviana" rises audibly as Blanche enters the bedroom.)

5 BLANCHE *(with faintly hysterical vivacity)*. I have just washed my hair.

STELLA. Did you?

BLANCHE. I'm not sure I got the soap out.

EUNICE. Such fine hair!

10 BLANCHE *(accepting the compliment)*. It's a problem. Didn't I get a call?

STELLA. Who from, Blanche?

BLANCHE. Shep Huntleigh . . .

STELLA. Why, not yet, honey!

15 BLANCHE. How strange! I —

(At the sound of Blanche's voice Mitch's arm supporting his cards has sagged and his gaze is dissolved into space. Stanley slaps him on the shoulder.)

STANLEY. Hey, Mitch, come to!

20 *(The sound of this new voice shocks Blanche. She makes a shocked gesture, forming his name with her lips. Stella nods and looks quickly away. Blanche stands quite still for some moments – the silverbacked mirror in her hand and a look of sorrowful perplexity as*

25 *though all human experience shows on her face. Blanche finally speaks with sudden hysteria.)*

---

1 **amber:** bernsteinfarben.
2 **radiance:** Glanz.
3 **sculptural:** plastisch.
17 **to sag:** sich senken, sinken.
17 f. **to be dissolved into space:** ins Leere gehen.
19 **to come to:** zu sich kommen.
23 **silverbacked:** mit silberner Rückseite.
24 **perplexity:** Verwirrung.

BLANCHE. What's going on here?
(She turns from Stella to Eunice and back to Stella. Her
rising voice penetrates the concentration of the game.
Mitch ducks his head lower but Stanley shoves back his
5 *chair as if about to rise. Steve places a restraining hand*
on his arm.)
BLANCHE *(continuing).* What's happened here? I want an
explanation of what's happened here.
STELLA *(agonizingly).* Hush! Hush!
10 EUNICE Hush! Hush! Honey.
STELLA. Please, Blanche.
BLANCHE. Why are you looking at me like that? Is some-
thing wrong with me?
EUNICE. You look wonderful, Blanche. Don't she look
15 wonderful?
STELLA. Yes.
EUNICE. I understand you are going on a trip.
STELLA. Yes, Blanche *is.* She's going on vacation.
EUNICE. I'm green with envy.
20 BLANCHE. Help me, help me get dressed!
STELLA *(handing her dress).* Is this what you —
BLANCHE. Yes, it will do! I'm anxious to get out of here –
this place is a trap!
EUNICE. What a pretty blue jacket.
25 STELLA. It's lilac coloured.
BLANCHE. You're both mistaken. It's Della Robbia blue.

---

5 **to restrain:** zurückhalten.
9 **agonizingly** (adv.): qualvoll.
18 **vacation:** Urlaub (AE).
25 **lilac:** Flieder; fliederfarben.
26 **Della Robbia blue:** helles Blau (etwas röter und dunkler als das Blau
von Vergißmeinnicht; benannt nach der italienischen Bildhauerfami-
lie Della Robbia aus dem 15. Jh.).

The blue of the robe in the old Madonna pictures. <u>Are</u>
<u>these grapes washed?</u>
(She fingers the bunch of grapes which Eunice has
brought in.)

5 EUNICE. Huh?

BLANCHE. Washed, I said. Are they washed?

EUNICE. They're from the French Market.

BLANCHE. That doesn't mean they've been washed. *(The*
cathedral bells chime.) Those cathedral bells – they're
10   the only clean thing in the Quarter. Well, I'm going
now. I'm ready to go.

EUNICE *(whispering)*. She's going to walk out before they
get here.

STELLA. Wait, Blanche.

15 BLANCHE. I don't want to pass in front of those men.

EUNICE. Then wait'll the game breaks up.

STELLA. Sit down and . . .

(Blanche turns weakly, hesitantly about. She lets them
push her into a chair.)

20 BLANCHE. I can smell the sea air. The rest of my time I'm
going to spend on the sea. And when I die, I'm going to
die on the sea. You know what I shall die of? *(She*
plucks a grape.) I shall die of eating an unwashed grape
one day out on the ocean. I will die – with my hand in
25   the hand of some nice-looking ship's doctor, a very
young one with a small blond moustache and a big
silver watch. "Poor lady," they'll say, "the quinine did
her no good. That unwashed grape has transported her

---

9 **to chime:** läuten.
18 **hesitantly** (adv.): zögernd.
26 **moustache:** Schnurrbart.
27 **quinine:** Chinin.

soul to heaven." *(The cathedral chimes are heard.)*
And I'll be buried at sea sewn up in a clean white sack
and dropped overboard – at noon – in the blaze of
summer – and into an ocean as blue as *(chimes again)*
5 my first lover's eyes!
*(A Doctor and a Matron have appeared around the
corner of the building and climbed the steps to the
porch. The gravity of their profession is exaggerated –
the unmistakable aura of the state institution with its
10 cynical detachment. The Doctor rings the doorbell. The
murmur of the game is interrupted.)*
EUNICE *(whispering to Stella)*. That must be them.
(Stella presses her fist to her lips.)
BLANCHE *(rising slowly)*. What is it?
15 EUNICE *(affectedly casual)*. Excuse me while I see who's at
the door.
STELLA. Yes.
(Eunice goes into the kitchen.)
BLANCHE *(tensely)*. I wonder if it's for me.
20 *(A whispered colloquy takes place at the door.)*
EUNICE *(returning, brightly)*. Someone is calling for
Blanche.
BLANCHE. It *is* for me, then! *(She looks fearfully from one
to the other and then to the portières. The "Var-
25 souviana" faintly plays.)* Is it the gentleman I was
expecting from Dallas?

---

6 **matron:** Oberschwester.
8 **gravity:** Ernst.
  exaggerated: übertrieben.
9 **unmistakable:** unfehlbar, unverkennbar.
  aura: (fig.) Atmosphäre, Ausstrahlung, Wirkung.
  state institution: staatliche Institution.
10 **detachment:** Distanz, Abstand.
20 **colloquy:** Gespräch.

EUNICE. I think it is, Blanche.

BLANCHE. I'm not quite ready.

STELLA. Ask him to wait outside.

BLANCHE. I . . .

5   *(Eunice goes back to the portières. Drums sound very softly.)*

STELLA. Everything packed?

BLANCHE. My silver toilet articles are still out.

STELLA. Ah!

10 EUNICE *(returning)*. They're waiting in front of the house.

BLANCHE. They! Who's "they"?

EUNICE. There's a lady with him.

BLANCHE. I cannot imagine who this "lady" could be! How is she dressed?

15 EUNICE. Just – just a sort of a – plain-tailored outfit.

BLANCHE. Possibly she's — *(Her voice dies out nervously.)*

STELLA. Shall we go, Blanche?

BLANCHE. Must we go through that room?

20 STELLA. I will go with you.

BLANCHE. How do I look?

STELLA. Lovely.

EUNICE *(echoing)*. Lovely.

(Blanche moves fearfully to the portières. Eunice draws
25   *them open for her. Blanche goes into the kitchen.)*

BLANCHE *(to the men)*. Please don't get up. I'm only passing through.

(She crosses quickly to outside door. Stella and Eunice follow. The poker players stand awkwardly at the table
30   *– all except Mitch, who remains seated, looking at the*

---

15 **plain-tailored:** einfach geschneidert.

*table. Blanche steps out on a small porch at the side of
the door. She stops short and catches her breath.)*

DOCTOR. How do you do?

BLANCHE. You are not the gentleman I was expecting.
5 *(She suddenly gasps and starts back up the steps. She
stops by Stella, who stands just outside the door, and
speaks in a frightening whisper.)* That man isn't Shep
Huntleigh.

(The "Varsouviana" is playing distantly.

10 *Stella stares back at Blanche. Eunice is holding Stella's
arm. There is a moment of silence — no sound but that of
Stanley steadily shuffling the cards.*

*Blanche catches her breath again and slips back into the
flat. She enters the flat with a peculiar smile, her eyes*
15 *wide and brilliant. As soon as her sister goes past her,
Stella closes her eyes and clenches her hands. Eunice
throws her arms comfortingly about her. Then she
starts up to her flat. Blanche stops just inside the door.
Mitch keeps staring down at his hands on the table, but*
20 *the other men look at her curiously. At last she starts
around the table towards the bedroom. As she does,
Stanley suddenly pushes back his chair and rises as if to
block her way. The Matron follows her into the flat.)*

STANLEY. Did you forget something?   hostile

25 BLANCHE *(shrilly).* Yes! Yes, I forgot something!
*(She rushes past him into the bedroom. Lurid re-
flections appear on the walls in odd, sinuous shapes.
The "Varsouviana" is filtered into weird distortion, ac-*

---

16 **to clench:** fest zusammenpressen.
28 **to be filtered into s.th.:** hier: sich langsam zu etwas verändern.
    weird: unheimlich.
    distortion: Verzerrung.

companied by the cries and noises of the jungle. Blanche seizes the back of a chair as if to defend herself.)

STANLEY. Doc, you better go in.

5 DOCTOR *(motioning to the Matron).* Nurse, bring her out. *(The Matron advances on one side. Stanley on the other. Divested of all the softer properties of womanhood, the Matron is a peculiarly sinister figure in her severe dress. Her voice is bold and toneless as a fire-*

10 *bell.)*

MATRON. Hello, Blanche.
(The greeting is echoed and re-echoed by other mysterious voices behind the walls, as if reverberated through a canyon of rock.)

15 STANLEY. She says that she forgot something.
(The echo sounds in threatening whispers.)

MATRON. That's all right.

STANLEY. What did you forget, Blanche?

BLANCHE. I – I —

20 MATRON. It don't matter. We can pick it up later.

STANLEY. Sure. We can send it along with the trunk.

BLANCHE *(retreating in panic).* I don't know you – I don't know you. I want to be – left alone – please!

MATRON. Now, Blanche!

25 ECHOES *(rising and falling).* Now, Blanche – now, Blanche – now, Blanche!

STANLEY. You left nothing here but spilt talcum and old

---

5 **to motion to s.o.:** jdm. etwas (durch Zeichen) bedeuten.
7 **divested:** (fig.) entkleidet, bar.
   property: Eigenschaft.
13 **to reverberate:** (Schall) zurückwerfen.
14 **canyon:** Schlucht.
27 **talcum:** Körperpuder.

empty perfume bottles – unless it's the paper lantern you want to take with you. You want the lantern?

(He crosses to dressing-table and seizes the paper lantern, tearing it off the light bulb, and extends it towards her. She cries out as if the lantern was herself. The Matron steps boldly towards her. She screams and tries to break past the Matron. All the men spring to their feet. Stella runs out to the porch, with Eunice following to comfort her, simultaneously with the confused voices of the men in the kitchen. Stella rushes into Eunice's embrace on the porch.)

STELLA. Oh, my God, Eunice help me! Don't let them do that to her, don't let them hurt her! Oh, God, oh, please God, don't hurt her! What are they doing to her? What are they doing? *(She tries to break from Eunice's arms.)*

EUNICE. No, honey, no, no, honey. Stay here. Don't go back in there. Stay with me and don't look.

STELLA. What have I done to my sister? Oh, God, what have I done to my sister?

EUNICE. You done the right thing, the only thing you could do. She couldn't stay here; there wasn't no other place for her to go.

(While Stella and Eunice are speaking on the porch the voices of the men in the kitchen overlap them.)

STANLEY *(running in from the bedroom)*. Hey! Hey! Doctor! Doctor, you better go in!

DOCTOR. Too bad, too bad. I always like to avoid it.

PABLO. This is a very bad thing.

STEVE. This is no way to do it. She should've been told.

PABLO. *Madre de Dios! Cosa mala, muy, muy mala!*

---

31 **Madre de Dios! Cosa mala, muy, muy mala!** (Span.): Mutter Gottes! Schlimme Sache, ganz, ganz schlimm!

(Mitch has started towards the bedroom. Stanley cross-
es to block him.)

MITCH *(wildly)*. You! You done this, all o' your God
damn interfering with things you —

5 STANLEY. Quit the blubber! *(He pushes him aside.)*

MITCH. I'll kill you! *(He lunges and strikes at Stanley.)*

STANLEY. Hold this bone-headed cry-baby!

STEVE *(grasping Mitch)*. Stop it, Mitch.

PABLO. Yeah, yeah, take it easy!

10 *(Mitch collapses at the table, sobbing.*
During the preceding scenes, the Matron catches hold
of Blanche's arm and prevents her flight. Blanche turns
wildly and scratches at the Matron. The heavy woman
pinions her arms. Blanche cries out hoarsely and slips
15 *to her knees.)*

MATRON. These fingernails have to be trimmed. *(The*
Doctor comes into the room and she looks at him.)
Jacket, Doctor?

DOCTOR. Not unless necessary.

20 *(He takes off his hat and now becomes personalized.*
The unhuman quality goes. His voice is gentle and
reassuring as he crosses to Blanche and crouches in
front of her. As he speaks her name, her terror subsides
a little. The lurid reflections fade from the walls, the
25 *inhuman cries and noises die out and her own hoarse*
crying is calmed.)

---

5 **blubber** (infml.): Geflenne, Gejammer.
6 **to lunge at s.o.:** sich auf jdn. stürzen.
7 **bone-headed** (infml.): blöde, doof.
  cry-baby (infml.): Heulsuse.
16 **to trim:** (kurz) schneiden.
18 **jacket:** *straitjacket:* Zwangsjacke.
20 **to become personalized:** zur Person werden.

DOCTOR. Miss DuBois.
(She turns her face to him and stares at him with desper-
ate pleading. He smiles; then he speaks to the Matron.)
It won't be necessary.

5 BLANCHE *(faintly)*. Ask her to let go of me.

DOCTOR *(to the Matron)*. Let go.
(The Matron releases her. Blanche extends her hands
towards the Doctor. He draws her up gently and sup-
ports her with his arm and leads her through the por-
10 *tières.)*

BLANCHE *(holding tight to his arm)*. Whoever you are – I
have always depended on the kindness of strangers.
(The poker players stand back as Blanche and the Doc-
tor cross the kitchen to the front door. She allows him to
15 *lead her as if she were blind. As they go out on the*
porch, Stella cries out her sister's name from where she
is crouched a few steps upon the stairs.)

STELLA. Blanche! Blanche, Blanche!
(Blanche walks on without turning, followed by the
20 *Doctor and the Matron. They go around the corner of*
the building.
Eunice descends to Stella and places the child in her
arms. It is wrapped in a pale blue blanket. Stella accepts
the child, sobbingly. Eunice continues downstairs and
25 *enters the kitchen where the men except for Stanley, are*
returning silently to their places about the table. Stanley
has gone out on the porch and stands at the foot of the
steps looking at Stella.)

STANLEY *(a bit uncertainly)*. Stella?
30 *(She sobs with inhuman abandon. There is something*

---

30 **with abandon:** mit Leib und Seele.

*luxurious in her complete surrender to crying now that
her sister is gone.)*

STANLEY *(voluptuously, soothingly).* Now, honey, Now,
love. Now, now love. *(He kneels beside her and his*
5   *fingers find the opening of her blouse.)* Now, now,
love. Now, love. . . .
*(The luxurious sobbing, the sensual murmur fade away
under the swelling music of the "blue piano" and the
muted trumpet.)*
10 STEVE. This game is seven-card stud.

---

3 **voluptuously** (adv.): sinnlich.
   soothingly (adv.): besänftigend.
7 **sensual:** sinnlich.
9 **muted:** gedämpft.

Editorische Notiz

Der englische Text folgt der Ausgabe: *Four Plays by Tennessee Williams*, London: Secker & Warburg, 1957, S. 65–154. Das Glossar erklärt in der Regel alle Wörter, die über die Wertigkeitsstufe 4 des *Englischen Arbeitswörterbuches* von Alfred Haase (Frankfurt a. M.: Moritz Diesterweg, [7]1979) hinausgehen. Im Zweifelsfall wurde großzügig verfahren, d. h. eher eine Vokabel mehr aufgenommen als dort vorgesehen.

Der Text weist zahlreiche Wörter und Phrasen der Umgangssprache und des Slangs auf, die im Glossar als solche gekennzeichnet sind. Vornehmlich die Sprache Stanleys, Mitchs und Eunices ist voller umgangssprachlicher grammatikalischer Konstruktionen oder Kurzformen – typisch für alle Dialekte und Soziolekte des Englischen. Hierzu gehören folgende Phänomene:

1. *Kontraktionen*

gotta: got to; have got to.
ain't: aren't; haven't.

2. *Doppelte Verneinung als einfache Verneinung*

You don't have to look no further: You don't have to look any further.
You won't pick up nothing: You won't pick up anything.

3. *Inkongruenz zwischen Person und Endung*

We was playing: We were playing.
She don't go: She doesn't go.
I hopes: I hope.
Where is the clothes?: Where are the clothes?
That's don't make no difference: That doesn't make any difference.
Wasn't we: Weren't we.

4. *Adjektiv statt Adverb*

real sweet: really sweet.
awful hard: awfully hard.

5. *Verwechslung von Pronomina*

What's them?: What are those?
of them papers: of those papers.
them darn: those darn.

6. *»Like« statt »as« oder »such as«*

You been exercising hard like bowling is: You have been
  exercising hard such as bowling is.

7. *Lexische Fehler*

I said to hush up: I told you to hush up.

8. *Konjugationsfehler*

are took in: are taken in.
She give me this: She gave me this.

9. *Wortauslassungen*

What number you looking for?: What number are you looking
  for?
Where you from?: Where are you from?
Have a shot?: Do you want to have a shot?
When you been exercising: When you have been exercising.
How long you here for?: How long are you going to be here for?
That she come here: That she has come here.

Im Glossar verwendete Abkürzungen

adv.	adverb
AE	American English
arch.	archaic (veraltet)
fig.	figuratively (übertragen)
Fr.	French
Gr.	Greek
hum.	humorously (scherzhaft)
infml.	informal (umgangssprachlich)
iron.	ironically
o.s.	oneself
pej.	pejorative (abwertend)
pl.	plural
poet.	poetical (dichterisch, gehoben)
prov.	proverbial (sprichwörtlich)
sing.	singular
s.o.	someone
Span	Spanish
s.th.	something

Anmerkungen

1 Der stark vom Imagismus geprägte amerikanische Dichter
   Hart Crane (1899–1932) beging aus Verzweiflung über
   seine vermeintlich schwindenden literarischen Fähigkeiten
   Selbstmord, vielleicht auch wegen seiner homosexuellen
   Neigungen und seiner Trunksucht.

2 In der griechischen Mythologie ist Elysium der Aufenthalt
   der Seligen nach dem Tod, wie etwa in Vergil, *Aeneis*, Buch
   6, Z. 637–751 beschrieben.

3 Eine der wichtigsten Ursprungsformen des Jazz. Charakte-
   ristisch für diese Musik sind v. a. die »blue notes« (die er-
   niedrigte dritte, siebte und gelegentlich fünfte Stufe: Blues-
   Terz, Blues-Septime, »flatted fifth«); hierdurch kommt es
   im Blues zu der charakteristischen Vermischung von Dur
   und Moll. Zur Rolle der Musik vgl. Nachwort.

4 Beiname des zypriotischen Leviten Josef, der den Apostel
   Paulus auf seiner ersten Missionsreise begleitete.

5 Der amerikanische Dichter Edgar Allan Poe (1809–49) ist
   als Verfasser von unheimlichen, grausigen und bizarren
   Kurz- und Kriminalgeschichten berühmt geworden.

6 Der Witz basiert vermutlich auf dem Wortspiel *mass* ›Mes-
   se‹ bzw. ›Körper‹, so daß der Polizist verstellt: »Guckt schon
   etwas von dem Körper heraus?«

7 Beginn einer populären amerikanischen Ballade. Text: N. R.
   Eberhart (1871–1944); Musik: Ch. W. Cadman (1881–1946).

8 Anspielung auf die aufwendigen, mit viel Glanz in Szene
   gesetzten Produktionen aus Amerikas Filmmetropole Hollywood bei Los Angeles.

9 Anderer Ausdruck für »bop« oder »bebop«, eine Form des
   Jazz, die sich durch rhythmische und harmonische Komple-
   xität sowie ihren innovativen Charakter auszeichnet und deren Melodien auf unsinnige Silben und Worte gesungen
   werden.

10 Ekstatische und emotionale Jazzmusik voll komplexer
   Rhythmen und kontrapunktischer Improvisationen.

11 Poker kann auch mit Jokern oder anderen wilden Karten in der Funktion von Jokern gespielt werden. Einäugige Buben sind im französischen Kartenspiel der Karo-Bube, im internationalen Bridge-Blatt, dem hier benutzten, der Herz-Bube und der Pik-Bube.

12 Beim Stud-Poker gibt es keinen Karten-Tausch; ein Teil der Karten wird mit der Bildseite nach oben gegeben, alle Karten bleiben auf dem Tisch liegen. Beim Sieben-Karten-Stud werden die erste, zweite und die siebte Karte verdeckt, die dritte bis sechste offen auf den Tisch gelegt.

13 Der aus Spanien stammende kubanische Bandleader Xavier Cugat (1900–87) popularisierte in den vierziger Jahren kubanische Musik in den USA.

14 Bei diesem Spiel erhält jeder Spieler »vier Karten, die – wie stets beim Poker – einzeln gegeben werden. Die folgende Karte wird offen, also mit der Bildseite nach oben, in die Tischmitte gelegt. Alle Karten von gleichem Wert wie die Tischkarte gelten als wild, die Tischkarte ebenfalls. Jeder Spieler betrachtet die offene Tischkarte als seine fünfte, aber niemand nimmt sie auf.« (Claus D. Grupp, *Alles über Pokern*, Niedernhausen (Taunus): Falken-Verlag, 1978, S. 76 f.).

15 Das Zitat stammt aus dem vorletzten Gedicht (Nr. 43) von Elizabeth Barrett Brownings (1806–61) Sonettzyklus *Sonnets from the Portuguese* (1850). In diesen Sonetten kommt die Liebe der Dichterin zu ihrem Ehemann, dem Dichter Robert Browning, zum Ausdruck. Der komplette Text des Gedichts lautet:

> »How do I love thee? Let me count the ways.
> I love thee to the depth and breadth and height
> My soul can reach, when feeling out of sight
> For the ends of being and ideal Grace.
> I love thee to the level of everyday's
> Most quiet need, by sun and candle-light.
> I love thee freely, as men strive for Right;
> I love thee purely, as they turn from Praise.
> I love thee with the passion put to use

In my old griefs, and with my childhood's faith.
I love thee with a love I seemed to lose
With my lost saints, – I love thee with the breath,
Smiles, tears, of all my life! – and, if God choose,
I shall but love thee better after death.«

16 Vierzehnzeiliges Gedicht provenzalisch-italienischen Ursprungs; sehr weit verbreitet in der englischen Literatur, seit Sir Thomas Wyatt (1503–42) und Henry Howard, Earl of Surrey (um 1517- 47) 1547 erstmals Gedichte auf englisch (meist Übersetzungen von Petrarca-Gedichten) veröffentlichten. Das Reimschema von Sonetten folgt zwei Grundmustern: abba/abba//cde/dce oder abab/cdcd/efef//gg.

17 Louisiana, ehemals spanischer und französischer Besitz und nach Louis XIV benannt, ist seit 1812 amerikanischer Bundesstaat und hat eine starke französische Minderheit, darunter auch Nachfahren der Hugenotten, den französischen Protestanten, von denen ein Teil bereits im 16. Jh. nach Florida auswanderte, um der Verfolgung durch den französischen Staat zu entgehen. In Louisiana stellen die Nachfahren der Hugenotten unter der französisch-stämmigen Bevölkerung eine Minderheit dar.

18 Der aus Neuengland stammende Autor Nathaniel Hawthorne (1804–64) ist besonders bekannt für seinen Roman *The Scarlet Letter* (1850) und die Kurzgeschichtensammlungen *The House of the Seven Gables* (1851) und *Twice-Told Tales* (1837).

19 Das Hauptwerk des amerikanischen Dichters Walt Whitman (1819–92) ist die in elf Ausgaben erschienene, immer wieder neu bearbeitete und ergänzte Gedichtsammlung *Leaves of Grass*.

20 »Paper Doll« ist der Titel eines in Millionenauflage verkauften populären Schlagers der Mills Brothers aus dem Jahr 1943.

21 Der Biscayne Boulevard ist eine der Hauptstraßen von Miami am Golf von Biscayne im amerikanischen Bundesstaat Florida.

22 Von der Mitte eines Quadrats mit der Seitenlänge 30 Yards

wirft ein Werfer einen Ball, der von einem Fänger, einem an
einer Ecke des Quadrats, dem Wurfmal, stehenden Spieler
mit einem Schläger innerhalb eines Sektors in Verlänge-
rung der das Wurfmal begrenzenden Quadratseiten weg-
geschlagen werden muß. Gelingt dies, darf der Fänger das
Quadrat im Gegenzeigersinn umlaufen und dabei jede
Ecke (1., 2., 3. Mal) berühren, bis die Mannschaft des Wer-
fers den Ball zu ihren an den Malen postierten Spielern zu-
rückgeworfen und einer von ihnen den laufenden Spieler
oder mit dem Ball ein Mal berührt hat. Erreicht der Fänger das dritte Mal, erhält seine Mannschaft einen Punkt,
und der Fänger wird gewechselt.

23 Die Ziege gilt in der klassisch-griechischen Mythologie als
Symbol der Fruchtbarkeit und Sexualität; daher die Be-
zeichnung »goat« für einen Mann (vgl. etwa im Deutschen
»geiler Bock«).

24 Anspielung auf die bekannte Oper *Der Rosenkavalier*
(1911) von Richard Strauss (1864–1949).

25 Dieser See begrenzt New Orleans im Norden und ist durch
einen Kanal mit dem Mississippi verbunden, der zwischen einem halben und etwa sieben Metern höher liegt als der See.

26 Die amerikanische Filmschauspielerin Mae West (1892 bis
1980), bekannt für ihre beträchtliche Oberweite, ist ein
Sexsymbol der dreißiger und vierziger Jahre.

27 Der griechische Ausruf geht auf Archimedes zurück, der
ihn bei der Entdeckung des archimedischen Prinzips (Vo-
lumenmessung eines unregelmäßigen Körpers durch Mes-
sen der verdrängten Wassermenge) benutzt haben soll.

28 In dem Roman *La Dame aux Camélias* (1848) von Alexan-
dre Dumas dem Jüngeren (1824–95) geht es um die echte
Liebe der ehemaligen Dirne Marguerite Gautier zu dem
aus vornehmer Familie stammenden Armand Duval, ihre
Opferbereitschaft und ihren Tod an der Schwindsucht.

29 »It' Only a Paper Moon« ist der Titel einer Jazz-Komposi-
tion von Harold Arlen, Billy Rose und E. Y. Harburg aus
dem Jahr 1932, bekanntgeworden durch Aufnahmen von
Nat King Cole, Ella Fitzgerald, Lionel Hampton u. v. a.

30 Der amerikanische demokratische Politiker Huey Pierce
Long (1893–1935) war von 1928 bis 1931 Gouverneur und
von 1931 bis 1935 Senator von Louisiana. Bekannt für seine
antikapitalistischen Tendenzen und seine diktaturähnliche
Herrschaft, wurde er 1935 ermordet.

31 Anspielung auf die schwierige und verlustreiche Landung
von 169 000 alliierten Soldaten bei Salerno (südlich von Nea-
pel) gegen harten deutschen Widerstand am 8./9. September
1943.

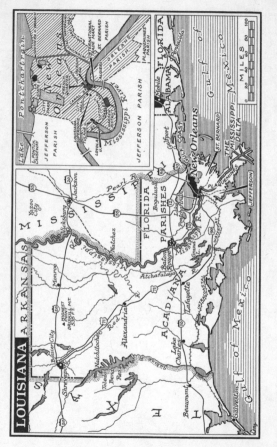

Lageplan von New Orleans. (Aus: Neal R. Peirce, *The Deep South States of America. People, Politics, and Power in the Seven Deep South States*, New York: Norton, 1974, S. 49.)

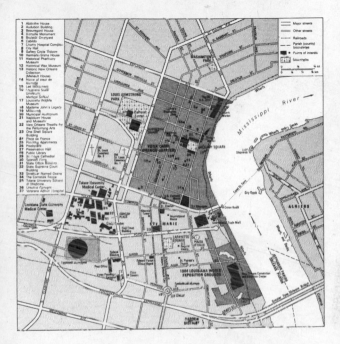

Plan der Innenstadt von New Orleans. (Aus: *The Encyclopedia Britannica*, Macropaedia, Bd. 13, Chicago 1974.)

Literaturhinweise

Adler, Thomas P., »*A Streetcar Named Desire*«: *The Myth and the Lantern*, Boston 1990.

Amerikanische Dramaturgie, hrsg. von H. Frenz und C. Clüver, Reinbek 1962.

Das amerikanische Drama von den Anfängen bis zur Gegenwart, hrsg. von Hans Itschert, Darmstadt 1972.

The American South, hrsg. von Louis D. Rubin Jr., Baton Rouge 1980.

Asibong, Emmanuel B., *Tennessee Williams: The Tragic Tension*, Ilfracombe 1978.

Asselineau, Roger, »Tennessee Williams ou la Nostalgie de la Pureté«, in: *Etudes Anglaises* 10 (1957) S. 431–443.

Berkman, Leonhard, »The Tragic Downfall of Blanche Du Bois«, in: *Modern Drama* 10 (1967) S. 249–257.

Bigsby, C. W. E., *A Critical Introduction to Twentieth-Century Drama*, Bd. 2, Cambridge 1984.

– »Tennessee Williams: Streetcar to Glory«, in: *The Forties: Fiction, Poetry, Drama*, hrsg. von W. G. French, Sydney 1969, S. 251–258.

Blackwell, Louise, »Tennessee Williams and the Predicament of Women«, in: *South Atlantic Bulletin* 35 (1970) S. 9–14.

Brown, Cecil, »Interview with Tennessee Williams«, in: *Partisan Review* 45 (1978) S. 276–305.

Buchloh, Paul G., »Tennessee Williams: Assoziationschiffren. Zeichen der Verweisung und Akzentuierung – Versuch einer Systematisierung«, in: *Studien zur englischen und amerikanischen Sprache und Literatur: Festschrift für Helmut Papajewski*, hrsg. von Paul G. Buchloh, Inge Leimberg und Herbert Reuter, Neumünster 1974, S. 405–439.

Buell, John, »The Evil Imagery of Tennessee Williams«, in: *Thought* 38 (1963) S. 167–189.

Chesler, S. Alan, »*A Streetcar Named Desire*: Twenty-five Years of Criticism«, in: *Notes on Mississippi Writers* 7 (1974) S. 44–53.

Confronting Tennessee Williams' »A Streetcar Named Desire«: Essays in Critical Pluralism, hrsg. von Philip C. Kolin, London 1993.

Corrigan, Mary Ann, »Memory, Dream, and Myth in the Plays of Tennessee Williams«, in: *Renascence* 28 (1976) S. 155–167.

– »Realism and Theatricalism in *A Streetcar Named Desire*«, in: *Modern Drama* 19 (1976) S. 385–396.

Costello, Donald P., »Tennessee Williams' Fugitive Kind«, in: *Modern Drama* 15 (1972) S. 26–43.

Davis, Joseph K., »The American South as Mediating Image in the Plays of Tennessee Williams«, in: *Amerikanisches Drama und Theater im 20. Jahrhundert*, hrsg. von Alfred Weber und Siegfried Neuweiler, Göttingen 1975, S. 171–189.

Donahue, Francis, *The Dramatic World of Tennessee Williams*, New York 1964.

Dowling, Ellen, »The Derailment of *A Streetcar Named Desire*«, in: *Literatur / Film Quarterly* 9 (1981) S. 233–240.

Downing, Robert, »Streetcar Conductor: Some Notes from Backstage«, in: *Theater Annual* 8 (1950) S. 25–33.

Durham, Frank, »Tennessee Williams, Theatre Poet in Prose«, in: *South Atlantic Bulletin* 36 (1971) S. 3–16.

England, Gene, »The Unacceptable Present, the Unobtainable Past: A Recurrent Theme in the Works of Tennessee Williams«, in: *Indiana English Journal* 7 (1973) S. 46–52.

Falk, Signi L., *Tennessee Williams*, New Haven (Conn.) 1961.

Fedder, Norman J., *The Influence of D. H. Lawrence on Tennessee Williams*, Den Haag 1966.

Fischer-Seidel, Therese, *Mythenparodie im modernen englischen und amerikanischen Drama*, Heidelberg 1986.

Foster, Verna, »Desire, Death, and Laughter: Tragicomic Dramaturgy in *A Streetcar Named Desire*«, in: *American Drama* 9 (1999) S. 51–58.

Frenz, Horst / Weisstein, Ulrich, »Tennessee Williams and His German Critics«, in: *Symposium* 14 (1960) S. 258–275.

Friedrich, Jutta, »Individuum und Gesellschaft in den Dramen von Tennessee Williams«, in: *Zeitschrift für Amerikanistik und Anglistik* 13 (1965) S. 45–60.

Fritscher, John J., »Some Attitudes and a Posture: Religious Metaphor and Ritual in Tennessee Williams' Query of the American God«, in: *Modern Drama* 13 (1970) S. 201–215.

Ganz, Arthur, »The Desperate Morality of Tennessee Williams«, in: *American Scholar* 31 (1962) S. 278–294.

Gassner, John, »*A Streetcar Named Desire*, a Study in Ambiguity. Excerpt from *The Theatre in Our Times*«, in: *Modern Drama. Essays in Criticism*, hrsg. von T. M. Bogard und W. J. Oliver, New York 1965, S. 374–385.

– »Tennessee Williams: Dramatist of Frustration«, in: *College English* 10 (1948) S. 1–7.

Griffin, Alice, *Understanding Tennessee Williams*, Columbia (S. C.) 1995.

Groene, Horst, »Tennessee Williams im Zwiespalt der Meinungen: Ein Forschungsbericht über die englisch- und deutschsprachige Literatur zu Williams' dramatischem Werk«, in: *Literatur in Wissenschaft und Unterricht* 5 (1972) S. 66–87.

Hainsworth, J. D., »Tennessee Williams: Playwright«, in: *Etudes Anglaises* 20 (1967) S. 225–232.

Hayman, Ronald, *Tennessee Williams: Everyone Else Is an Audience*, New Haven (Conn.) 1993.

Hays, Peter L., »Arthur Miller and Tennessee Williams«, in: *Essays in Literature* 4 (1977) S. 239–249.

Heilman, Robert, »Tennessee Williams: Approaches to Tragedy«, in: *Southern Review* N. F. 1 (1965) S. 770–790.

Hethman, Robert, »The Foul Rag-and-Bone Shop of the Heart«, in: *Drama Critique* 8 (1965) S. 94–102.

Hirsch, Foster, *A Portrait of the Artist: The Plays of Tennessee Williams*, London 1979.

Hurley, Paul J., »Tennessee Williams: The Playwright as Social Critic«, in: *Theater Annual* 21 (1964) S. 40–56.

Iwamoto, Iwao, »Truth and Illusion in the Plays of Tennessee Williams«, in: *Studies in English Literature* (Tokio) 41 (1964) S. 73–86.

Jackson, Esther Merle, *The Broken World of Tennessee Williams*, Madison 1965.

Jackson, Esther Merle, »Music and Dance as Elements of Form in the Drama of Tennessee Williams«, in: *Revue d'Histoire du Théâtre* 15 (1963) S. 294–302.

– »The Problem of Form in the Drama of Tennessee Williams«, in: *College Language Association Journal* 4 (1960) S. 8–21.

Jausslin, Christian M., *Tennessee Williams*, Velber 1969.

Jones, Robert Emmet, »Tennessee Williams' Early Heroines«, in: *Modern Drama* 2 (1959) S. 211–219.

Kazan, Elia, »Notebook for *A Streetcar Named Desire*«, in: *Directors on Directing*, hrsg. von T. Cole und H. K. Chinoy, Indianapolis 1963, S. 364–379.

Kernan, Alvin B., »Truth and Dramatic Mode in the Modern Theater: Chekhov, Pirandello, and Williams«, in: *Modern Drama* 1 (1958) S. 101–114.

Kolin, Philip C. [u. a.], »*A Streetcar Named Desire*: A Playwright's Forum«, in: *Michigan Quarterly Review* 29 (1990) S. 175–203.

Link, Franz H., *Tennessee Williams' Dramen: Einsamkeit und Liebe*, Darmstadt 1974.

Machts, Walter, »Das Menschenbild in den Dramen Tennessee Williams'«, in: *Die Neueren Sprachen* 10 (1961) S. 445–455.

Magid, Marion, »The Innocence of Tennessee Williams«, in: *Commentary* 25 (1963) S. 34–43.

Maxwell, G., *Tennessee Williams and Friends*, Cleveland (N. Y.) 1965.

Mennemeier, Franz Norbert, »Tennessee Williams«, in: F. N. M., *Das moderne Drama des Auslandes*, Düsseldorf ³1976, S. 66–80.

Nelson, Benjamin, *Tennessee Williams: The Man and His Work*, New York 1961.

Nordon, Pierre, »Le jeu des stéréotypes dans *Un Tramway Nommé Désir*«, in: *Etudes Anglaises* 32 (1979) S. 154–161.

Oppel, Horst, »›Every Man is a King!‹ Zur Funktion der lokalhistorischen Elemente in *A Streetcar Named Desire*, in: *Studien zur englischen und amerikanischen Sprache und*

Literatur: Festschrift für Helmut Papajewski, hrsg. von Paul G. Buchloh, Inge Leimberg und Herbert Reuter, Neumünster 1974, S. 507–522.

da Ponte, Duran, »Tennessee Williams' Gallery of Feminine Characters«, in: *Tennessee Studies in Literature* 10 (1965) S. 7–26.

Popkin, Henry, »The Plays of Tennessee Williams«, in: *Tulane Drama Review* 4 (1960) S. 45–64.

Porter, Thomas E., *Myth and Modern American Drama*, Detroit 1969.

Riddel, Joseph N., »*A Streetcar Named Desire* – Nietzsche Descending«, in: *Modern Drama* 5 (1963) S. 421–430.

Rogers, Ingrid, *Tennessee Williams: A Moralist's Answer to the Perils of Life*, Frankfurt a. M. 1976.

Rogoff, Gordon, »The Restless Intelligence of Tennessee Williams«, in: *Tulane Drama Review* 10 (1966) S. 78–92.

Sackstedter, William, »The Three Cats: A Study in Dramatic Structure«, in: *Drama Survey* 5 (1966) S. 252–266.

Sagar, Keith M, »What Mr. Williams Has Made of D. H. Lawrence«, in: *Twentieth Century* 168 (1960) S. 143–153.

Savran, David, »›By Coming Suddenly Into a Room That I Thought Was Empty‹: Mapping the Closet with Tennessee Williams«, in: *SLI* 24 (1991) S. 57–74.

Schlueter, June, »Imitating an Icon: John Erman's Remake of Tennessee Williams' *A Streetcar Named Desire*«, in: *Modern Drama* 28 (1985) S. 139–147.

Sharp, William, »An Unfashionable View of Tennessee Williams«, in: *Tulane Drama Review* 6 (1962) S. 160–171.

Spevack, Marvin, »Tennessee Williams: The Idea of the Theater«, in: *Jahrbuch für Amerikastudien* 10 (1965) S. 221–231.

von Szeliski, John, »Tennessee Williams and the Tragedy of Sensitivity«, in: *Western Humanities Review* 20 (1966) S. 203–211.

Tennessee Williams: A Collection of Critical Essays, hrsg. von Stephen S. Stanton, Englewood Cliffs (N. J.) 1977.

Tennessee Williams: A Tribute, hrsg. von Jack Tharpe, Jackson 1977.

Thompson, Judith J., *Tennessee Williams' Plays: Memory, Myth and Symbol*, New York 1987.

Tischler, Nancy M., »The Distorted Mirror: Tennessee Williams' Self-Portraits«, in: *Mississippi Quarterly* 25 (1972) S. 389–403.

– *Tennessee Williams, Rebellious Puritan*, New York 1961.

Twentieth-Century Interpretations of »A Streetcar Named Desire«, hrsg. von Jordan Y. Miller, Englewood Cliffs (N. J.) 1971.

Vahland, Barbara, *Der Held als Opfer. Aspekte des Melodramatischen bei Tennessee Williams*, Frankfurt a. M. 1976.

Weales, Gerald, *Tennessee Williams*, Minneapolis 1965.

Weissman, Philip, »Psychopathological Characters in Current Drama. A Study of a Trio of Heroines«, in: *American Imago* 17 (1960) S. 271–288.

Zuber, Ortrun, »The Translation of Non-Verbal Signs in Drama«, in: *Pacific Quarterly* 5 (1980) S. 61–74.

Nachwort

I

Fast genau drei Jahre nach seinem Durchbruch am Broadway mit *The Glass Menagerie*, das ihm den begehrten Preis des New York Critics' Circle einbrachte,[1] übertraf Tennessee Williams mit seinem Stück *A Streetcar Named Desire* diesen ersten Erfolg noch ganz erheblich: 855 Aufführungen[2] en suite folgten der New Yorker Premiere am 3. Dezember 1947; Williams erhielt den Kritiker-Preis erneut und dazu den Pulitzer-Preis.[3] Aus dem scheuen, zurückhaltenden sechsunddreißigjährigen Dramatiker war durch diese zwei Dramen eine gefeierte, nationale Größe[4] geworden – von vielen mit Amerikas bis dahin führendem Dramatiker des 20. Jahrhunderts Eugene O'Neill (1888 bis 1953) auf eine Stufe gestellt.

Gleichwohl mischten sich schon unter die ersten, überwiegend sehr positiven Besprechungen des Dramas in seiner Erstinszenierung durch Elia Kazan[5] und mit den Schauspielern Jessica Tandy als Blanche, Kim Hunter als Stella, Karl Malden als Mitch und Marlon Brando als Stanley kritische Töne. Unstrittig war lediglich der Publikumserfolg der Inszenierung: »It is [, .] highly successful theatre and highly successful showmanship«, räumte George Jean Nathan, ein einflußreicher Kritiker ein,[6] und Brooks Atkinson urteilte elf Tage nach der Premiere in *The New York Times*:

1 Vgl. die Chronologie zum Leben Williams' in: *Twentieth Century Interpretations of »A Streetcar Named Desire«*, hrsg. von Jordan Y. Miller, Englewood Cliffs (N. J.) 1971, S. 111.
2 Vgl. Bernhard Reitz, »Nachwort«, in: Tennessee Williams, *The Glass Menagerie*, hrsg. von B. R., Stuttgart 1984, S. 139 (Reclams Universal-Bibliothek 9178).
3 Vgl. *Twentieth Century Interpretations*, S. 111.
4 Vgl. Jordan Y. Miller, »Introduction«, in: *Twentieth Century Interpretations*, S. 6.
5 Unter der Produktionsleitung von Irene Selznik besorgte Kazan auch die Regie der Hollywood-Verfilmung des Dramas mit Vivien Leigh in der Rolle der Blanche und ansonsten unveränderter Besetzung.
6 George, Jean Nathan, »Review of *A Streetcar Named Desire*, in: *Two Modern American Tragedies*, hrsg. von John D. Hurrell, New York 1961, S. 90.

»[People] come away from it profoundly moved and also in
some curious way elated. For they have been sitting all evening in the presence of truth, and that is a rare and wonderful
experience. Out of nothing more esoteric than interest in
human beings, Mr. Williams has looked steadily and wholly
into the private agony of one lost person.«[7]

Andererseits jedoch verglich Nathan das Stück mit einem Preis-
boxkampf oder einer Zirkusvorstellung; um »critically secure
drama«[8] handele es sich keineswegs: »While it may shock the
emotions of its audience, [it] does not in the slightest shock them
into any spiritual education«.[9] Auch schon Atkinson konsta-
tierte in seiner Besprechung die Weigerung des Dramatikers,
Position zu beziehen[10] oder das Publikum explizit zu bestimmten sozialen Wertungen anzuhalten. Dies, so meinten manche
der Erstrezensenten, stelle eine der zentralen Schwächen des
Stückes dar. Die Figuren ergäben sich kampflos der Übermacht
des feindlichen Schicksals.[11] Nur der Kampf des Individuums
gegen das Geschick mache hingegen das eigentlich Dramatische
aus:

»Great drama [. . .] arises from genuine conflict, an element
that can only be generated by the writer's conviction that the
battle is vital and the means to wage it exist. Williams will
write greatly only if he can re-examine reality and emotion-
ally recognize what his intellect may already have grasped:
that the forces of good in this world are adult and possess both
the will and the power to change our environment.«[12]

So zeichneten sich mit der ambivalenten Deutung der Bühnen-

7 Brooks Atkinson, »*Streetcar* Tragedy – Mr. Williams' Report on Life in New Orleans«, in: *Twentieth Century Interpretations*, S. 32; vgl. auch aus der gleichen
   Sammlung Howard Barnes, »O'Neill Status Won by Author of *Streetcar*«, S. 34,
   Joseph Wood Krutch, »Review of *Streetcar Named Desire*«, S. 38, und John Ma-
   son Brown, »Southern Discomfort«, S. 41.
8 Nathan (Anm. 6) S. 90; vgl. auch S. 89.
9 Ebd., S. 89.
10 Vgl. Atkinson (Anm. 7) S. 32.
11 Vgl. Richard Watts Jr., »*Streetcar Named Desire* Is Striking Drama«, in: *Twentieth Century Interpretations*, S. 31.
12 Harry Taylor, »The Dilemma of Tennessee Williams« (1948), in: *Two Modern
   American Tragedies*, S. 99.

wirksamkeit, dem Hinweis auf die angeblich fehlende Einbe-
ziehung der sozialen Dimension und der Kritik an seiner –
wie es hieß – pessimistischen Weltsicht bereits unmittelbar
nach dem spektakulären Broadway-Erfolg drei wichtige The-
men ab, die auch in der Folgezeit die Williams-Rezeption mit-
bestimmten.

II

Oft finden sich in der Kritik Hinweise auf Williams' Biographie
als Erklärungen für die in seinen Stücken enthaltene Weltsicht.
Aufgewachsen zwischen der mitfühlenden und empfindsamen
Mutter aus einer gebildeten Pfarrersfamilie aus dem Staat Mississippi und dem geschäftlich erfolgreichen, prosaischen und
gefühllosen Vater, der seine Mißbilligung der künstlerischen
Ambitionen seines ältesten Sohnes offen zum Ausdruck
brachte, indem er ihm den Abschluß seines Studiums verwehrte
und ihn statt dessen zur Arbeit als Verkäufer in einer Schuhfa-
brik zwang,[13] habe der Dramatiker Williams früh menschliches
Scheitern und menschliche Not – vor allem im Schicksal seiner
psychisch kranken Schwester Rose – erfahren. So habe das
Schreiben für Williams schon im Alter von vierzehn Jahren the-
rapeutischen Charakter besessen, indem es ihm die Flucht aus
einer als »uncomfortable« empfundenen Welt ermöglichte.[14]
Seine Weltsicht sei stark von seiner Biographie beeinflußt und
finde ihren Niederschlag in seinem Werk.[15] Daher seien seine
Dramen gekennzeichnet von Verzweiflung, Angst und Hoff-
nungslosigkeit,[16] aber auch von Mitgefühl für die Gescheiterten

---

13 Vgl. Miller (Anm. 4) S. 1 f.
14 Williams' eigene Aussage; hier zit. nach: John T. von Szeliski, »Tennessee
   Williams and the Tragedy of Sensitivity«, in: *Twentieth Century Interpretations*,
   S. 67.
15 Vgl. Jutta Friedrich, »Individuum und Gesellschaft in den Dramen von Tennessee
   Williams«, in: *Zeitschrift für Amerikanistik und Anglistik* 13 (1965) S. 45.
16 Vgl. dazu Szeliski (Anm. 14) S. 67, Reitz (Anm. 2) S. 139, und Franz Norbert
   Mennemeier, *Das moderne Drama des Auslandes*, Düsseldorf 1976, S. 77.

und Versager[17] – für Laura Wingfield in *The Glass Menagerie* und Blanche in *A Streetcar Named Desire*.

Ist es schon grundsätzlich mehr als fraglich, ob ein Kritiker ohne weiteres biographische Details eines Autors auf dessen Werk übertragen darf, weil ein solches Verfahren nur zu leicht den Blick auf die Individualität des Werks verstellt, so kommt in Williams' Fall noch hinzu, daß die Zeit der endgültigen Abfassung von *A Streetcar Named Desire* nach seinem eigenen Bekunden und trotz seiner Befürchtung, an Krebs erkrankt zu sein, zu den glücklichen zu zählen ist:

> »Grandfather was a wonderful traveling companion. . . . Just being with him revived my own pleasure in the fact of existence.
>
> We arrived in Key West and occupied a two-room suite on the top of the Hotel La Concha and it was there that I really began to get *Streetcar* into shape. It went like a house on fire, due to my happiness with Grandfather.«[18]

Selbst wenn man also von der Gültigkeit des biographischen Ansatzes überzeugt wäre, böte sich dieses Zitat nun nicht gerade an, um die These von der pessimistischen Weltsicht des Stücks *A Streetcar Named Desire* zu stützen. Erst eine genaue Analyse des Dramas selbst kann klären, ob die Figuren tatsächlich hilflos einem feindlichen Geschick ausgeliefert sind, das sie vernichtet, oder ob sie in der Lage sind, entweder das zerschmetterte Universum zu heilen[19] oder zumindest gegen ihr Schicksal anzukämpfen.

Während diese Kritik an der angeblich negativen Weltsicht des Dramas von der Notwendigkeit einer sozusagen propagandistischen Botschaft eines literarischen Werks ausgeht, machen andere Autoren ideologische oder normativ-dramentheoretische Einwände gegen das Stück geltend. So hält Desmond Reid

---

17 Vgl. Roger Asselineau, »Tennessee Williams ou la Nostalgie de la Pureté«, in: *Das amerikanische Drama von den Anfängen bis zur Gegenwart*, hrsg. von Hans Itschert, Darmstadt 1972, S. 292.

18 Tennessee Williams, *Memoirs*, Garden City 1975, S. 111; zu seiner Krebs-Angst vgl. S. 110.

19 Vgl. Esther Merle Jackson, *The Broken World of Tennessee Williams*, Madison 1965, S. 27.

(1957) die mangelnde Eigenverantwortlichkeit der Figuren für
»morally indefensible«;[20] Jutta Friedrich (1965) wirft Williams
vor, statt sozialem Protest gegen den Kapitalismus »Flucht in
den Subjektivismus«[21] geboten zu haben; seine autobiographisch verankerten Figuren seien »Selbstbildnisse eines Neurotikers«;[22] Horst Oppel (1974) endlich schließt seine umfassende
und gründliche Analyse des Stücks mit der Frage, ob Blanche –
und damit dem Drama – »die Würde des Tragischen, die stets
nur aus der Freiheit der Einsicht und der Entscheidung
erwächst, zugestanden werden kann.«[23]
Wieder andere Autoren finden in *A Streetcar Named Desire*
vornehmlich die unterschiedlichsten Oppositionsmuster. Die
Beziehung zwischen Stan und Blanche wird etwa als Aufeinanderprall von Dionysischem und Appollinischem im Sinne
Nietzsches,[24] von amerikanischem Norden und Süden,[25]
Wirklichkeit und Illusion,[26] Unkultur und Kultur,[27] Brutalität und Dekadenz,[28] physischen Bedürfnissen und Idealis

20 Desmond Reid, S. J., »Tennessee Williams« (1957), in: *Two Modern American Tragedies*, S. 104.

21 Friedrich (Anm. 15) S. 58.

22 Ebd., S. 60; zu psychoanalytischen Deutungen vgl. etwa Joseph N. Riddel, »A Streetcar Named Desire – Nietzsche Descending«, in: *Modern Drama* 5 (1962), S. 425, W. David Sievers, »Tennessee Williams and Arthur Miller« (1955), in: *Two Modern American Tragedies*, S. 139, Philip Weissman, »A Trio of Tennessee Williams' Heroines: The Psychology of Prostitution«, in: *Twentieth Century Interpretations*, S. 57–64.

23 Horst Oppel, »Tennessee Williams. A Streetcar Named Desire«, in: *Das amerikanische Drama*, hrsg. von Paul Goetsch, Düsseldorf 1974, S. 205.

24 Vgl. Riddel (Anm. 22) S. 428.

25 Vgl. Joseph K. Davis, »The American South as Mediating Image in the Plays of Tennessee Williams«, in: *Amerikanisches Drama und Theater im 20. Jahrhundert*, hrsg. von Alfred Weber und Siegfried Neuweiler, Göttingen 1975, S. 171–189, und Pierre Nordon, »Le Jeu des Stéréotypes dans *Un Tramway Nommé Désir*«, in: *Études Anglaises* 32 (1979) S. 161.

26 Vgl. Mary Ann Corrigan, »Realism and Theatricalism in *A Streetcar Named Desire*«, in: *Modern Drama* 19 (1976) S. 391, 393, und Alvin B. Kernan, »Truth and Dramatic Mode in the Modern Theater: Chekhov, Pirandello, and Williams«, in: *Modern Drama* 1 (1958) S. 111.

27 Vgl. Jürgen Koepsel, *Der amerikanische Süden und seine Funktionen im dramatischen Werk von Tennessee Williams*, Frankfurt a. M. 1974, S. 208.

28 Vgl. C. W. E. Bigsby, *A Critical Introduction to Twentieth-Century American Drama*, Bd. 2, Cambridge 1984, S. 67.

mus,[29] ja sogar von Leben und Tod[30] gesehen. Schon die Viel-
zahl solcher Deutungen ist ein Hinweis darauf, daß eine umfassende Analyse des Dramas sich nicht auf eine rein individualisti-
sche oder naturalistische Sicht festlegen darf. Die Figuren des
Stücks sind zwar sicher als Individuen eigenen Rechts im New
Orleans der späten vierziger Jahre zu verstehen, ihre Bedeutung geht jedoch weit darüber hinaus, und es wird letztlich zu
klären sein, ob sich diese Oppositionen zu einem überzeugen-
den Muster zusammenfügen.

III

Die unterschiedlichen Deutungen der Bühnenwirksamkeit des
Stückes schließlich hängen sowohl mit dem soeben angespro-
chenen Problem der Oppositionsmuster zusammen als auch –
und ganz besonders – mit Williams' Theaterkonzeption, die
zunächst und vordergründig naturalistisch erscheint.
Das Ehepaar Stella und Stan Kowalski bewohnt eines der typi-
schen weißen Holzhäuser mit Außentreppen in der Elysian
Fields Avenue am nordöstlichen Rande der Altstadt von New
Orleans, dem Vieux Carré, das zwar als Slum-Viertel beschrieben wird (S. 5), dem aber zugleich »raffish charm« und eine Art
von »lyricism« (ebd.) zugesprochen werden. Die von Blanche
erwähnten Straßenbahnlinien geben die jeweilige Endstation
an: das Stadtviertel Desire und »Friedhöfe« (S. 9). Das Haupt-
charakteristikum der Heimatstadt des Jazz – die Blues-Musik
aus den verschiedenen Jazz-Lokalen – ist überall zu hören (vgl.
S. 6 und 29). Das Rassengemisch dieser kosmopolitischen Stadt
wird als relativ unproblematisch beschrieben (vgl. S. 6), und
auch die schwül-warme Luft in New Orleans wird im Stück des
öfteren erwähnt (vgl. z. B. S. 26 f.).
Doch schon das ausgeprägte Lokalkolorit des Stückes ist nicht
bloß Teil eines naturalistischen Dramenkonzepts: Ortsnamen

29 Vgl. J. D. Hainsworth, »Tennessee Williams: Playwright on a Hot Tin Roof?«, in:
    Etudes Anglaises 20 (1967) S. 226.
30 Vgl. Nordon (Anm. 25) S. 159.

wie Elysian Fields, Desire und Cemeteries haben offensicht-
lich auch eine symbolische Funktion, und gleiches gilt für die
Namen der Figuren und der Plantage: Blanche DuBois und
Stella sind die letzten lebenden Mitglieder einer französisch-
stämmigen Pflanzerfamilie, wie sie für Louisiana und Missis-
sippi typisch ist, und der Name der Plantage ist französischen
Ursprungs. Zugleich aber wird das aristokratisch-französische
Erbe ironisch verfremdet: der schöne Traum (Belle Reve) –
grammatikalisch korrekt wäre: Beau Rêve – hat sich durch die
Dekadenz der DuBois, derer vom Walde, d. h. aus der Natur, in
Luft aufgelöst; die Unschuld[31] der älteren DuBois-Tochter ist
einer verzweifelten Promiskuität gewichen, und ob die jüngere
Tochter Stella ihrer durch den Namen suggerierten Leitstern-
funktion nachkommt, soll zunächst unbeantwortet bleiben.[32]
Auch hinsichtlich der Farben und Geräusche bzw. Musik ver-
fährt Williams ähnlich. Stan und seine Freunde tragen Hemden
in kräftigen, ungemischten Grundfarben (S. 45) und bevorzu-
gen das grelle Licht. Blanche hingegen trägt meist weiße Kleidung (S. 8 f. und 85)) und kann offenes Tageslicht oder das
Licht einer nackten Glühbirne nicht ertragen (S. 56 und 129 f.).
Akustisches Merkmal des Vieux Carré ist das »blue piano«;
Stans Kennzeichen sind die lärmende Kirmesmusik (S. 137), die
»Red hots«-Rufe des Tamale-Verkäufers (S. 44) und der Lärm
der nahenden Lokomotive (z. B. S. 145). Blanche andererseits
wird durch die Varsouviana, eine Polka, (S. 103 und 155) cha-
rakterisiert. Ungezügelte Gewalt, »primitive« Ursprünglichkeit
und selbstbewußte Extrovertiertheit werden so durch die farbli-
che und lautliche Gestaltung scharf von domestizierter Kraftlo-
sigkeit, überfeinerter Kultur und introvertierter Empfindsamkeit abgesetzt. Unter Ausnutzung der Plurimedialität[33] des
Theaters – auf der Bühne und im Film keineswegs als aufdring-
lich empfunden wie möglicherweise im Lesetext[34] – gelingt es

---

31 *blanche* (frz.): weiß (die Farbe der Unschuld).

32 Vgl. S. 193 ff. des Nachworts.

33 Vgl. Manfred Pfister, *Das Drama*, München 1977, S. 24–29.

34 Vgl. Oppel (Anm. 23) S. 202–204, Corrigan (Anm. 26) und Paul Gerhard Buch-
loh, »Gesellschaft, Individuum und Gemeinschaft bei Tennessee Williams«, in:
Das amerikanische Drama von den Anfängen bis zur Gegenwart (Anm. 17)
S. 319–322.

Williams, Individualität zu unterstreichen und zugleich symbolisch zu überhöhen.[35]

In der Ausnutzung der Darstellungsmöglichkeiten der Bühne geht Williams – wohl unter dem Einfluß von Erwin Piscator und Bertolt Brecht[36] – noch einen Schritt weiter. In der zehnten Szene wird die Hauswand transparent, um für Augenblicke einen Eindruck vom Leben auf der Straße zu vermitteln (S. 144); und der Zuschauer teilt mit Blanche das Erlebnis der quälenden Musik und der unheimlichen Schatten (S. 127 und 143 f.), die den anderen Bühnenfiguren verborgen bleiben. Auf diese Weise gibt Williams, die Regeln des naturalistischen Dramas durchbrechend und das Geschehen sozusagen episch kommentierend, einen Blick auf das Innenleben seiner Protagonistin frei, illustriert ihre existentielle Not und hebt doch gleichzeitig das Geschehen auf der Bühne über den konkreten Einzelfall hinaus, wie es auch seinem Programm eines »plastic theatre«, dem Versuch der Realisierung eines Gesamtkunstwerks,[37] entspricht:

> »Everyone should know nowadays the unimportance of the photographic art: that truth, life, or reality is an organic thing which the poetic imagination can represent or suggest, in essence, only through transformation, through changing into other forms than those which merely present in appearance.«[38]

Wenn man erkennt, daß Williams bühnentechnische und dramenspezifische Mittel nicht um ihrer selbst willen einsetzt, sondern um die existentielle Notlage Blanches angesichts der sie bedrängenden Realität dem Zuschauer manifest zu machen und ihn dadurch zu einer Stellungnahme zu zwingen,[39] wird man auch den Vorwurf der Sensationslüsternheit oder des bloßen Appells an das Gefühl nur als krasses Mißverständnis des Dra-

---

35 Vgl. etwa John Gassner, »Tennessee Williams: Dramatist of Frustration«, in: *College English* 10 (1948) S. 5.

36 Vgl. Jackson (Anm. 19) S. 91.

37 Vgl. Jackson, S. 108; auch S. 93, 94, 96.

38 Tennessee Williams, »Production Notes«, in: T. W., *The Glass Menagerie*, hrsg. von Bernhard Reitz, Stuttgart 1984, S. 8.

39 Vgl. Corrigan (Anm. 26) S. 395, und Kernan (Anm. 26) S. 113.

mas deuten müssen. Williams' »plastic theatre« dient dem Ziel, den Existenzkampf des Individuums in einer ihn bedrohenden Umwelt zu spiegeln:

> »For Williams, as for Dante, the theatre is by nature committed to an extremely important task. Its essential purpose is to show man the root of his suffering: its function, to play out humanity's crisis, to give its tortured consciousness concrete shape.«[40]

IV

Die Realität der modernen Welt, deren Anforderungen und Ansprüchen Blanche nicht gewachsen ist, wird in *A Streetcar Named Desire* verkörpert durch Stanley Kowalski, den in den USA geborenen Sohn einer polnischen Einwandererfamilie, der als Vertreter einer Maschinenfabrik arbeitet und sich seine freie Zeit vorwiegend beim Bowling oder mit Pokern vertreibt. Schon sein erster Auftritt läßt keinen Zweifel an Stans absolut dominierender Rolle in seiner Ehe mit Stella aufkommen. Wie in der primitiven Jägergesellschaft der Urmenschen ist Stan der unumschränkte Herrscher in seinem Bereich, dessen Pflichten ausschließlich die materielle Versorgung und die Fortpflanzung seiner Familie umfassen: Stanley bringt seiner Frau ein Paket Fleisch – die Jagdbeute – nach Hause (S. 7), fürchtet, von Blanche um Stellas und folglich sein Erbe betrogen worden zu sein (S. 39 f.) und hat alleinige Verfügungsgewalt über die Finanzen der Familie (S. 30, 71). In einer langen Bühnenanweisung schildert Williams Stan als »richly feathered male bird among hens« (S. 25).

Stans Vitalität, Nationalbewußtsein (S. 121) und Gastfreundschaft, der Stolz auf seine Manneskraft (»gaudy seed-bearer«, S. 25), sein zupackender Realismus und seine scharfe Beobachtungsgabe werden von Williams zunächst durchaus positiv geschildert. Er ist voll animalischer Lebensfreude, und seine

---

40 Jackson (Anm. 19) S. 130; vgl. auch Corrigan, S. 385, 392.

Ehe mit Stella stellt beide Seiten vollauf zufrieden. Sexualität ist das einigende Band, das diese sozial so ungleichen Partner zusammenhält: »But there are things that happen between a man and a woman in the dark – that sort of make everything else seem – unimportant« (S. 72 f.). Stellas vage, fast mystische Sicht der Sexualität, die einen Vergleich mit D. H. Lawrence durchaus gestattet,[41] wird jedoch durch Stan in einer Weise relativiert, die diesem auf den ersten Blick so sympathischen Tausendsassa und Draufgänger negative Züge verleiht, die dem Zuschauer auch vor der Vergewaltigungsszene schon die unbedenkliche Identifikation mit Stan erschweren: Für ihn erschöpft sich die Wirkung der sexuellen Vereinigung in der Faszination von aufleuchtenden bunten Lampen (S. 120)! Schwerer wiegt jedoch der geradezu totalitäre Verfügungsanspruch Stans über Stella, seine Unbeherrschtheit, Gewalttätigkeit und Rücksichtslosigkeit. Nur oberflächlich könnte man ihn einen »gesund empfindenden, normalen Menschen«[42] nennen. Unter der Maske des »normalen« Menschen kommt für kurze Augenblicke immer wieder der gedankenlose, oberflächliche, egozentrische Western-Held oder der typische Macho in der Art des Filmhelden Rambo zum Vorschein, die »base egotistical force, destructive of what it cannot comprehend«,[43] die ihren stärksten Ausdruck in der Vergewaltigung Blanches in der zehnten Szene findet.

Hier entwickeln sich die Ereignisse nach Stans vergeblichem Versöhnungsversuch mit seiner Schwägerin rasch in für Blanche höchst bedrohlicher Weise – vom Dramatiker vornehmlich durch optische und akustische non-verbale Zeichen kommentiert: »Lurid reflections appear on the walls around Blanche. The shadows are of a grotesque and menacing form« (S. 143), das Lokomotiv-Geräusch tritt auf, »the inhuman jungle voices rise up« (S. 145), und Stan beißt sich auf die Zunge, »which protrudes between his lips« (S. 146). Unmenschlichkeit, ja Bestialität charakterisieren diese Szene, in der sich sozusagen

41 Vgl. dazu etwa Krutch (Anm. 7) S. 137.
42 Friedrich (Anm. 15) S. 60.
43 Corrigan (Anm. 26) S. 393.

das Tiermännchen sein Weibchen nimmt – effektvoll unterstrichen von der »hot trumpet« und den lauten Trommeln der Jazz-Musik. So wenig Blanche in der Lage ist, sich sinnvoll mit der Realität zu arrangieren, so wenig ist Stan in der Lage, unter der Oberfläche nackter Fakten die Existenzangst Blanches wahrzunehmen. Für ihn ist sie bloß die verfügbare Sexualpartnerin, der gegenüber auch skrupellos Gewalt angewendet werden darf. Die Welten Stans und Blanches sind unvereinbar.

Um dem Zuschauer jedoch das sich gegen Ende des Stückes aufdrängende Grundmuster: Stan = schlecht, Blanche = gut fragwürdig zu machen, verändert der Dramatiker die Perspektive noch einmal. An der fundamentalen Ablehnung der realen Welt Stans wegen ihrer Brutalität gegenüber den Schwachen und Unangepaßten läßt er zwar keine Zweifel aufkommen, doch hat diese Kritik keinen radikalen Bruch mit der Realität zur Folge: Die Ehe der Kowalskis besteht am Schluß des Stückes fort. Stella akzeptiert nicht nur die Darstellung Stans und den Rat Eunices: »Life has got to go on. No matter what happens, you've got to keep on going« (S. 149), sondern sie zeigt in der Schlußszene sich wieder eingenommen von der sexuellen Ausstrahlungskraft Stans. Das »blue piano« und die gedämpfte Trompete Stans überblenden das »luxurious sobbing« und das »sensual murmur« (S. 160) des Paares[44] mit seinem Kind und bringen so tentativ die Möglichkeit einer harmonischen Ordnung ins Spiel, die sich in der Zukunft, wenn auch nicht in der Gegenwart realisieren könnte. Für den Augenblick bleibt den Beteiligten nur, ihr Leben fortzusetzen, als sei nichts geschehen: »The game is seven-card stud« (S. 160) oder in Stans Worten, die seine Lebensmaxime enthalten: »To hold front position in this rat-race you've got to believe you are lucky« (S. 148).

---

44 Im Gegensatz zum Bühnentext trennt sich Stella im Film von Stan. Ob diese Trennung von Dauer sein wird, bleibt allerdings offen, weil sie nur zu ihrer Nachbarin Eunice geht.

V

Das eben angesprochene Oppositionsmuster trifft aber auch deshalb nicht zu, weil Blanche, Stans Gegenspielerin, von Williams geradezu als Komplementärfigur, als weibliches Gegenstück mit umgekehrten Vorzeichen konzipiert ist. Bereits die Bühnenanweisung zu Blanches erstem Auftritt hinterläßt den Eindruck von Verletzlichkeit, Zerbrechlichkeit und emotionaler Angespanntheit (S. 8 f.) unter der eleganten, äußeren Erscheinung. Blanche, die scheinbar so gebildete, feine Dame aus einer – so scheint es – reichen Pflanzerfamilie aus Mississippi, büßt schon durch ihre ersten Handlungen einiges von der Sympathie des Zuschauers ein: Unverblümt besteht sie gegenüber der freundlichen, hilfsbereiten Eunice darauf, allein gelassen zu werden (S. 11); heimlich trinkt sie noch vor der Ankunft ihrer Schwester Stella ein halbes Wasserglas voll Whisky, stellt Glas und Flasche sorgfältig wieder an ihren Platz und beginnt unmittelbar nach der fieberhaften und hektischen Begrüßung Stellas (S. 13) die lange Reihe ihrer Täuschungen, indem sie vorgibt, den Whisky gerade erst zu entdecken. So unbedeutend dieses Detail auch erscheinen mag, so wichtig ist es für die Bewertung Blanches. In all ihrem Tun und all ihren Worten muß deutlich unterschieden werden zwischen ihrer Wirklichkeit und dem Bild, das sie von sich vermittelt, zwischen Realität und Illusion. Der Schmuck, den sie trägt, ist billigster Modeschmuck; die Bildung, die sie für sich beansprucht, ist nie einem wirklichen Test ausgesetzt; sie ist sechs Jahre älter, als sie vorgibt (S. 9, 56); sie verbirgt den Grund für ihr Erscheinen in New Orleans und täuscht Stan und Stella hinsichtlich ihres reichen Freundes Shep Huntleigh. Ihr ganzes Wesen scheint, oberflächlich betrachtet, auf Lüge und Betrug aufgebaut, im Unterschied zu Stan, der als Mann der harten, beweisbaren Fakten auftritt.

Aber wie Williams durch geschickte Akzentsetzung sicherstellte, daß Stan weder als normaler, sympathischer Durchschnittsamerikaner noch bloß als brutaler, unzivilisierter Rohling aufgefaßt werden darf, so stellt er durch entsprechende

Perspektivierung die Figur der Blanche äußerst differenziert
dar. Krasse moralische Bewertungen wie »simpering, witless
prostitute«,[45] medizinische Diagnosen wie »schizoid«, »schizo-
phren« oder »mentally unhinged«[46] sind ebenso unangemessen
wie Emporstilisierungen zur Personifikation der Kunst[47] oder
der Unschuld und Reinheit.[48]

Im Verlaufe des Stückes gestattet Williams dem Zuschauer
zunehmend Einblicke in das Innerste Blanches – er enthüllt ihre
immer verzweifelter werdenden Versuche, die moderne Welt
Stans mit der verlorengegangenen Welt ihrer unschuldigen, rei-
nen Vergangenheit, die Realität mit der Illusion in Deckung zu
bringen: »Yes, yes, magic! I try to give that to people. I misrepresent things to them. I don't tell truth, I tell what ought to be
truth« (S. 130); und er zeigt Blanches vergebliche Suche nach
Halt und Geborgenheit:[49] bei Stella und Stan, bei Mitch (S. 86),
dem jungen Mann (S. 87 f.), bei Shep Huntleigh und schließlich
sogar bei dem Anstaltsarzt.

Zu Beginn des Dramas vermittelt Blanches Verhalten den Eindruck der Unangemessenheit und Fragwürdigkeit; ihre emotionale Verfassung muß vom Zuschauer aus wenigen Symptomen
erschlossen werden. Gegen Ende des Stückes teilt das Publikum
Blanches Perspektive explizit und exklusiv, d. h. für die anderen Bühnenfiguren nicht erkennbar.[50] Zu den impliziten Bele-
gen für ihre Verfassung zählt dabei das Baderitual Blanches: es
impliziert physische und emotionale Reinigung; auch die Lie-
der, die sie beim Baden singt, machen unter der Oberfläche der
Fröhlichkeit und Unbeschwertheit das Bewußtsein des illusio-
nären Charakters ihrer Identität hörbar – »paper moon«, »card-

---

45 Watts (Anm. 11) S. 31.
46 Riddel (Anm. 22) S. 425, Friedrich (Anm. 15) S. 47 und C. W. E. Bigsby, »Tennessee Williams: Streetcar to Glory« (1969), in: *Twentieth Century Interpretations*, S. 106.
47 Vgl. Harold Clurman, »Review of *A Streetcar Named Desire*«, in: *Two Modern
   American Tragedies*, S. 93.
48 Vgl. Asselineau (Anm. 17) S. 282.
49 Vgl. Robert Emmet Jones, »Tennessee Williams' Early Heroines«, in: *Modern
   Drama* 2 (1959) S. 214.
50 Vgl. Abschnitt III des Nachworts.

board sea«, »make-believe« (S. 107), »Barnum and Bailey«, »phony«, »honky-tonk«, »penny arcade« (S. 108) –; die Varsouviana erklingt gegen Ende der achten und zu Beginn der neunten Szene »with sinister rapidity« (S. 124 f.).

In der neunten und zehnten Szene schließlich teilen der Zuschauer und Blanche die gleiche Wahrnehmungsperspektive und damit die quälende Erinnerung an den von Blanche mitverschuldeten Selbstmord ihres homosexuellen Mannes, dessen w a h r e Veranlagung sie unter dem S c h e i n des Künstlerischen nicht hatte erkennen können und den sie – in einem Augenblick der Gefühllosigkeit – angewidert zurückgewiesen hatte: »›I know! I know! You disgust me . . .‹« (S. 103 f.).[51] In dieser Situation hat sie sich auf die faktische Welt der Realität eingelassen, hat unter der Oberfläche der Tatsachen nicht die existentielle Not ihres Mannes gefühlt und ist dadurch – auch im aristotelischen Sinn[52] – tragisch schuldig geworden. Das Stück dokumentiert daher ihre vergeblichen Versuche, sowohl diese Schuld zu sühnen als auch in der Welt wieder Fuß zu fassen. In diesem Sinn muß auch ihre spätere Promiskuität gedeutet werden – nicht als Zeichen moralischer Prinzipienlosigkeit oder Dekadenz, sondern als Ausdruck ihrer panischen Suche nach Halt: »I think it was panic, just panic, that drove me from one to another, hunting for some protection« (S. 131).

Der Schluß des Dramas zeigt mit der Einlieferung Blanches in eine Nervenheilanstalt weniger ihre kampflose Niederlage gegen die Mächte des feindlichen Geschicks als vielmehr eher ihren Sieg über eben diese Realität: Mit dem letztlich freiwilligen Rückzug in das Sanatorium erfüllt sie sich ihren Wunsch nach Frieden und Geborgenheit, wenn auch ironischerweise außerhalb der Welt der »Normalität«. Sie sieht in dem Arzt den langersehnten Beschützer, der ihr Halt gibt (»holding tight to his arm«, S. 159). Illusion und Wirklichkeit werden wieder eins:

---

51 Auch Blanches homosexueller Mann wird oft als ein Porträt von Tennessee Williams bezeichnet. Williams bekennt sich in seinen *Memoirs* offen zu seiner Veranlagung.

52 Vgl. etwa Leonard Berkman, »The Tragic Downfall of Blanche Du Bois«, in: *Modern Drama* 10 (1967/68) S. 257; aber vgl. auch Oppel (Anm. 23) S. 205.

»Whoever you are – I have always depended on the kindness of
strangers« (S. 159). Sie verläßt Stellas Haus nicht als gebro-
chene Geisteskranke, sondern mit Würde – selbst die Poker-
spieler erweisen ihr ihre Reverenz, indem sie bei ihrem Eintritt
aufstehen (S. 154), und sie kann sich in diesem Augenblick des
Mitgefühls der Zuschauer sicher sein.

In dem gleichen Maß, in dem Stanley allmählich an Sympathie und moralischer Statur einbüßt, gewinnt Blanche. Allerdings erscheint fraglich, ob sie wirklich als »undisputed moral
victor«[53] bezeichnet werden darf. Vielmehr scheint Williams
bewußt die Unvereinbarkeit zweier gleichermaßen unvoll-
kommener Welten darzustellen.[54] Weder Stan und die durch
ihn personifizierte moderne Welt bloßer Fakten, der Gefühls-
kälte und Gewalttätigkeit noch Blanche und ihre verletzliche
Welt der Vergangenheit, der überlebten Traditionen und Illu-
sionen, der »Reinheit und Unversehrtheit«[55] repräsentieren
eine »even remotely acceptable moral choice«.[56] Wenn Williams überhaupt Stellung bezieht, eine klare Aussage zugunsten irgendeiner der dargestellten Positionen macht, dann
könnte allenfalls Stella, der Hoffnungsstern, eine Lösung per-
sonifizieren.

VI

Doch auch Stella kann der Rang der Idealfigur nicht zugestanden werden. Sie, die jüngere Schwester Blanches, hat ganz
bewußt und radikal mit ihrer Vergangenheit gebrochen und sich
auf die moderne Welt Stans eingelassen, um die Ruhe und
Geborgenheit zu finden, der ihre Schwester vergeblich nach-
jagt. Zwar muß sie dabei in Kauf nehmen, sich Stan völlig unter-
zuordnen, seine gelegentlichen, gewalttätigen Ausbrüche zu

53 Corrigan (Anm. 26) S. 393.
54 Vgl. Jackson (Anm. 19) S. 137.
55 Oppel (Anm. 23) S. 197.
56 Jackson (Anm. 19) S. 137; vgl. auch Robert B. Heilman, »Tennessee Williams:
   Approaches to Tragedy«, in: *The Southern Review*, N.F.1 (1965) S. 771.

ertragen und auf alles zu verzichten, was sie mit den Traditionen und den gesellschaftlichen Normen ihrer Jugend verbindet (S. 19), aber sie empfindet ihre Lage nicht als in irgendeiner Weise verbesserungsbedürftig: »I'm not in anything I want to get out of« (S. 67). Mit Ruhe und Entschlossenheit begegnet sie den Versuchen ihrer Schwester, sie ihrem Mann zu entfremden. Sie weigert sich, in Stan einen Höhlenmenschen der Urzeit zu sehen (S. 74 f.) und sich zugunsten der Kultur und der Empfindsamkeit (»poetry and music«, »tenderer feelings«, S. 75) von Stanley abzukehren.

Von Williams wird Stellas gänzlicher Verzicht auf Geistiges, ihre Reduktion auf das Physische und Emotionale – unterstrichen durch die »comics« (S. 64), mit denen sie sich am Morgen nach der Poker-Party die Zeit vertreibt, als sei nichts geschehen – als Defizit dargestellt. Die Ruhe, die Stella in dieser Szene ausstrahlt, ist die Ruhe einer Narkose (S. 64), Resultat eines ausgeschalteten Bewußtseins. Stella hat auf alles Kulturelle verzichtet, auf Kunst, Musik, Literatur, Bildung, Umgangsformen, sie hat alles Traditionelle über Bord geworfen, um dafür einen »Gewinn an häuslicher Geborgenheit und sexueller Befriedigung«[57] zu erzielen, und der Preis, den sie dafür zu zahlen hat, ist hoch.

Die Erfüllung, die sie findet, ist begrenzt, aber sie ist andererseits auch durchaus real.[58] Die »eastern idols« (S. 64), von denen im Zusammenhang mit der »almost narcotized tranquillity« (S. 64) die Rede ist, erinnern nämlich auch an die mystische, transrationale Gelassenheit, Friedfertigkeit und Harmonie fernöstlicher Religionen. Stella kann ihre Gefühle für Stan nicht verbal, mit den Mitteln der Ratio definieren, sondern allenfalls umschreiben oder durch physischen Kontakt ausdrücken: »Oh, you can't describe someone you're in love with« (S. 20). »And when he comes back I cry on his lap like a baby« (S. 21). Ihr Wesen ist gekennzeichnet durch Sanftmut (»gentle«, S. 7), Zärtlichkeit (S. 62) und Mitgefühl mit den

57 Oppel (Anm. 23) S. 194.
58 Vgl. Hainsworth (Anm. 29) S. 226, und Buchloh (Anm. 34) S. 323.

Schwächen anderer. Daher ist es auch nur folgerichtig, daß sie sich am Schluß ihrem Mann nicht, wie es in der Kazan-Verfilmung geschieht, entzieht. Sie muß sich letztlich entscheiden zwischen ihrem Mitgefühl mit Blanche und ihrer Familie, und sie entscheidet sich für Stan und das Kind: »But in doing so she opts for the future over the past, for potency over sterility. And if that also means accepting a world bereft of protective myths and cultural adornments this is a compromise which she has the strength to make«.[59] Williams läßt somit den Ausgang des Stückes offen, er vermittelt dem Zuschauer Seinsweisen mit all ihren Vorzügen und Nachteilen, er löst die Widersprüche nicht auf, sondern verlangt vom Zuschauer, sich seinen Weg selbst zu suchen. Die Zukunft – in der Gestalt des Babys – ist noch unentschieden, ein positiver Ausgang ist zumindest nicht ausgeschlossen: »Stanley's vitality and Stella's compassion«[60] könnten den Schlüssel zur Lösung des Konflikts bedeuten.

VII

Vor diesem Hintergrund läßt sich nun auch die eingangs aufgeworfene Frage nach der Gültigkeit der verschiedenen Oppositionsmuster beantworten. Durch die Einbettung des Stückes in einen für den Zuschauer nachvollziehbaren zeitlichen und örtlichen Rahmen zwingt der Dramatiker sein Publikum, die Figuren zunächst als Individuen eigenen Rechts mit ganz spezifischen Problemen und Konflikten zu sehen; mit den Mitteln des »plastic theatre« jedoch erweitert er die Perspektive über den konkreten Einzelfall hinaus.[61] Die Traditionen und die Weltsicht der alten Pflanzeraristokratie der Südstaaten – der überlebte Mythos des »alten Südens« – gerät in Konflikt mit den Normen der modernen Massengesellschaft, der aktuellen Rea-

59 Bigsby (Anm. 28) S. 65 f.
60 Ebd., S. 62.
61 Vgl. Marvin Spevack, »Tennessee Williams: The Idea of the Theater«, in *Das amerikanische Drama von den Anfängen bis zur Gegenwart* (Anm. 17) S. 259.

lität der USA, wie er auch in anderen literarischen Werken des 20. Jahrhunderts, etwa W. Faulkners *Sartoris* (1929), darge- stellt wird. Allerdings wäre auch eine Sicht des Dramas als bloße Darstellung des Niedergangs der »moribund culture«[62] des amerikanischen Südens zu eng. Williams fügt dieser zeit- geschichtlichen Dimension noch eine andere, wichtigere hin- zu. Der Mensch muß sich seinen Weg suchen zwischen ele- mentfremden, unvereinbaren Welten, die sich doch – wie Stan und Blanche – komplementär ergänzen. Stan und die moderne Stadt New Orleans repräsentieren Fakten, Unkul- tur, Vermassung, Technik, Brutalität und Geschichtslosigkeit, aber gleichzeitig auch Vitalität, Kraft, Leben schlechthin; Blanche und der alte, ländliche Süden stehen für Illusion, Kultur, Individualität, Kunst und Sensibilität, aber zugleich auch für Labilität, Dekadenz, ja Tod.[63] Menschliche Existenz gelingt nur zwischen diesen beiden Polen und setzt Kompro- misse und Opfer voraus: »Offered a choice between decadence and brutality the audience can hardly enter into an alliance with either«.[64]

Es geht Williams nicht um das konkrete Einzelschicksal oder das Zeitgeschichtliche um seiner selbst willen, sondern um die Darstellung der Gefährdung der menschlichen Existenz schlechthin. Wie im alten *miracle play* exemplifiziert der kon- krete Einzelfall den kosmischen Konflikt:

> »In all, Williams is occupied with the simultaneity of, so to speak, the subliminal and the supraliminal. His anatomizing of the single soul is to lay bare the primordial condition: if the individual is scarred and neurotic, it is that the cosmos itself is scarred and neurotic. As in the old morality play, the outer drama mirrors the inner.«[65]

Dies ist die »Botschaft« von *A Streetcar Named Desire*, zu der sich alle Komponenten des Stückes – »design, word, gesture,

62 Corrigan (Anm. 26) S. 392; vgl. Koepsel (Anm. 27) S. 208.
63 Vgl. etwa Nordon (Anm. 25) S. 159.
64 Bigsby (Anm. 28) S. 67.
65 Spevack (Anm. 61) S. 262.

mime, music, dance, and light«[66] – zusammenfügen. Das Resultat ist ein Stück, das auch nach vierzig Jahren nichts von seiner Faszination eingebüßt hat und zu Recht zu den berühmtesten Dramen des 20. Jahrhunderts gezählt wird.

Herbert Geisen

66 Jackson (Anm. 19) S. 107.

Inhalt

Reclams Rote Reihe

▶ **Originaltexte fremdsprachiger Literatur**

ENGLISCH FRANZÖSISCH
ITALIENISCH RUSSISCH SPANISCH

Ungekürzt und unbearbeitet, mit der Übersetzung
schwieriger Wörter auf jeder Seite und einem
Nachwort mit Informationen zu Autor und Werk.

LATEIN

Die wichtigsten Werke der römischen Literatur in
Auswahlausgaben und Textsammlungen zu verschiedenen Themenbereichen. Ein Kommentar
am Fuß jeder Seite liefert die nötigen Sprach- und
Sacherläuterungen.

▶ **Sprachtraining**

Sprachen leichter lernen und Grammatikkennt-
nisse auffrischen mit den Sprachtrainingsbänden
aus Reclams Roter Reihe.

Das komplette Programm und Detailinforma-
tionen zu jedem Titel unter www.reclam.de